If Jesus Was a Project Manager

Faith-based Leadership *in a* Results-driven World

SHAWNA CALHOUN

LUCIDBOOKS

If Jesus Was a Project Manager:
Faith-based Leadership in a Results-driven World

Copyright © 2025 by Shawna Calhoun

Published by Lucid Books in Houston, TX
www.LucidBooks.com

All rights reserved. No part of this publication may be reproduced, stored in a retrieval system, or transmitted in any form by any means, electronic, mechanical, photocopy, recording, or otherwise, without the prior permission of the publisher, except as provided for by USA copyright law.

Unless otherwise indicated, scripture quotations are taken from the NKJV® Bible (New King James Version®). Copyright © 1982 by Thomas Nelson. Used by permission. All rights reserved.

ISBN: 978-1-63296-849-4
eISBN: 978-1-63296-850-0

Special Sales: Most Lucid Books titles are available in special quantity discounts. Custom imprinting or excerpting can also be done to fit special needs. Contact Lucid Books at Info@LucidBooks.com

*All glory goes to YAH, my God, my everything.
I would be nothing and could do nothing without Him.*

Contents

Introduction: Building God's Kingdom, One Project at a Time 1

Part I: The Foundation of Faith-Based Leadership 21
The most sophisticated project management methodologies mean nothing without godly leadership at the foundation. This part of the book establishes the biblical principles that transform ordinary project managers into servant leaders who reflect Christ's character in every interaction. We'll explore how Jesus's leadership style, the power of building authentic relationships, and leading with humility create the foundation for projects that not only succeed but transform lives and organizations.

Chapter 1: The Greatest Project Ever Undertaken 23

Chapter 2: Servant Leadership in Project Management 37

Chapter 3: Building Teams Like Jesus Built Disciples 45

Part II: Divine Project Planning 63
Even the most charismatic leader will fail without proper planning. This part of the book delves into how biblical principles transform traditional project planning methodologies. We'll discover how divine vision, providence-guided planning, and faith-based risk management create project plans that not only achieve earthly success but align with God's eternal purposes.

Chapter 4: Vision That Moves Mountains 65

Chapter 5: Planning with Providence 85

Chapter 6: Risk Management Through Faith 111

Part III: Leading Through Storms 139
Every project faces unexpected challenges, difficult stakeholders, and moments when failure seems inevitable. This part of the book equips Christian project managers with biblical strategies for navigating the inevitable storms of project leadership. Learn how Christ-centered communication, conflict resolution, and failure recovery can transform your most challenging projects into opportunities for spiritual growth and organizational breakthrough.

Chapter 7: Communication That Connects Hearts 141

Chapter 8: Conflict Resolution the Jesus Way 169

Chapter 9: When Projects Fail: Redemption and Restoration 199

Part IV: Finishing Strong **231**

The final phase of any project often determines whether temporary success becomes lasting impact. This part of the book focuses on delivering excellence that honors God, celebrates achievements appropriately, and builds a legacy that extends far beyond any single project. Discover how biblical principles of stewardship, gratitude, and mentorship can transform project closure into Kingdom building.

Chapter 10: Delivering Excellence for God's Glory 233

Chapter 11: Celebrating Success and Giving Glory 241

Chapter 12: Legacy Leadership 267

Afterword 291

Acknowledgments 305

Appendix A: Biblical Project Management Principles: Quick Reference 307

Appendix B: Prayers for Project Managers 329

About the Author 345

INTRODUCTION
Building God's Kingdom, One Project at a Time

But seek first the kingdom of God and His righteousness, and all these things shall be added to you.

—Matt. 6:33

Welcome to Faith Forward Life, where faith meets the workplace in practical, transformative ways. I'm Shawna Calhoun, and I created Faith Forward Life to help Christian professionals like you discover how your work is both your calling and your mission field.

Faith Forward Life serves as the home for my "Faith at Work" book series—starting with "If Jesus Was a Project Manager"—along with ongoing blog content that explores how we can exhibit the fruit of the Spirit in our daily business scenarios. Whether you're leading a team, managing projects, or navigating workplace challenges, this platform provides biblical wisdom and practical tools for living out your faith Monday through Friday.

I never set out to become a Christian project manager who writes books. My original plan was straightforward: excel in project management, complete my doctorate without losing my sanity, serve others faithfully, and maybe retire early to travel. God had different plans. Through years of managing projects—some successful, others that taught me humility—I've discovered that our greatest professional tool isn't just best practices or methodologies, but the transformative power of applying biblical principles to our work.

If you're a Christian professional who believes your workplace is more than just a paycheck, Faith Forward Life is for you. Together, we'll explore how to bring kingdom values into conference rooms, how to lead with Christ-like character, and how to see our Monday morning meetings as opportunities to shine His light.

The Call to Write and the Spiritual Battle

This book, the first in the *Faith at Work* series, didn't emerge from professional success alone. It was born from a divine calling that came with its own spiritual warfare. When the Lord first placed the vision for the series on my heart, I knew I was stepping into something that would challenge everything in me and around me. What I didn't anticipate was how fierce the battle would become or how God would use that battle to teach me to fly.

In late 2024, Sister Celestial—a true woman of God,

a woman of faith, and a true prophet of the Lord for such a time as this—warned us that 2025 would be a year of both unprecedented Kingdom opportunities and unprecedented spiritual turbulence. She used the phrase "2025: The year when the wheels fall off" to describe the level of disruption coming for many believers. While some would experience new business opportunities for furthering God's Kingdom, others would face trials that would either refine them like gold or break them entirely. I thought I was prepared for this prophetic word. I was wrong.

Sister Celestial, I want to take this moment to give you a heartfelt shout-out and express my deepest gratitude for your obedience to the Lord in delivering His Word with such accuracy and love. Your faithfulness in speaking truth, even when it was difficult to hear, prepared my heart for what was to come. May God continue to bless you mightily as you serve His people with the prophetic gift He has entrusted to you. Thank you for being a faithful vessel for His voice in such a time as this.

When the Wheels Fell Off–And God Grew Wings

Shortly after the year 2025 began, I experienced what seemed to be a simple burst water pipe in my home, but when I say the wheels fell off my God-accelerating car, I mean THE. WHEELS. FELL. OFF! It's like God's foot was on the gas pedal, and He removed any kind of brake pedal. What followed was a cascade of events that would test every project management principle I had ever learned—and every ounce of faith I possessed.

The water damage led to extensive flooding, which required major remodeling and construction that took months to complete. Construction delays, contractor issues, and insurance complications turned what should have been a straightforward restoration into a complex, multi-stakeholder nightmare. But that was just the beginning. In the midst of managing the chaos at home, devastating personal family situations emerged that left me emotionally shattered and spiritually questioning. Without going into details that would violate the privacy of those I love, I can say that I found myself in the valley of the shadow of death, walking through circumstances that broke my heart in ways I never knew were possible.

Yet through it all, life didn't pause. I continued working full-time as a healthcare information technology (IT) program manager, overseeing critical implementations that supported the quality of critical patient care. I pressed on with my doctoral studies in project management, submitting research papers while sitting in construction zones and processing grief that threatened to overwhelm me. I maintained my volunteer commitments with the Project Management Institute (PMI) as a subject matter expert, knowing that other professionals were counting on my expertise. I continued mentoring junior project managers and university students, pouring into their development even when I felt completely empty.

But here's what I discovered. When the wheels fell off, God didn't abandon the vehicle; He transformed it into something that could fly.

The Great Revelation (or How I Stopped Worrying and Learned to Love Faith-Based Project Management)

Just as eagles must face the fierce winds of the storm to learn to soar above it, God used the very turbulence that threatened to destroy me to teach me a new dimension of faith-based project management. When I could no longer rely on the familiar wheels of human strength, conventional wisdom, and predictable processes, the Holy Spirit began developing supernatural wings of divine insight, prophetic discernment, and Kingdom authority.

Let me start with a confession that might make some of my secular colleagues nervous and some of my Christian friends question my theology. I believe Jesus would have been an absolutely phenomenal project manager.

I know, I know. Before you start typing angry comments about reducing the Savior of the world to someone with a Project Management Professional (PMP) certification, hear me out. I'm not saying Jesus needed project management. I'm saying project management desperately needs Jesus.

The trials I was experiencing weren't obstacles to overcome. They were wind currents designed to lift me higher. Every construction delay became a lesson in divine timing.

Every insurance complication taught me about trusting God's provision. Every family crisis revealed deeper truths about stakeholder relationships and servant leadership. Every moment of emotional exhaustion pushed me to discover supernatural strength that could only come from above.

Through it all, the Holy Spirit was also leading me to finish writing this book in a way that so beautifully connects the dots.

Hindsight with Spiritual Eyes to See

With insight gained through spiritual eyes to see, I was able to discern a major turning point in my life that came during what I now call Project Nightmare 2022. (Names have been changed, and minor scenario edits were made to protect the innocent and avoid lawsuits.) I was managing a particularly challenging government-funded healthcare IT program where nothing was going according to plan. We were implementing a comprehensive health information exchange system that would connect multiple healthcare organizations across our West Coast region, enabling secure patient data sharing and improved care coordination.

The program was heavily dependent on a vendor partnership that was more one-sided than a toddler's conversation about dinosaurs. We did all the listening, and they responded to our issue escalations and attempted course corrections with the worst case of stonewalling and petulant silent treatments. They were like a customer service chatbot that pretended it didn't understand perfectly clear questions, responding only with "I'm sorry, I didn't catch that" while you slowly descend into madness, typing "speak to a human" in increasingly creative ways.

Three months into the program, we were behind schedule, over budget, and discovering that our strategic partner had oversold their capabilities by approximately the same margin that I had overestimated my ability to survive on three hours of sleep per night. The clinical staff was frustrated with system delays. The government oversight team was questioning every decision. Stakeholder meetings felt like exercises in creative excuse-making.

During one particularly tense program review, our Chief Information Officer (CIO) looked across the conference table (well, it was actually the camera since it was a teleconference meeting, but you know what I mean) and asked a question that stopped everyone cold. "Are we managing this program, or is this program managing us?"

The Moment Everything Changed

That night, I found myself in my office at 11:00 p.m., staring at program plans that seemed to mock my decade-plus experience and multiple certifications. I had all the right methodologies, the latest project management software, and a team of competent professionals. Yet somehow we were failing to deliver on our most fundamental responsibility: improving patient care through better information sharing.

In that moment of professional desperation, I did something I'd never done before. I started praying about my project. It wasn't just "God, please don't let this be a complete disaster" prayer but I was actually seeking wisdom for specific decisions, asking for patience with difficult stakeholders, and requesting discernment about when to escalate issues.

For years, I had operated under the assumption that my faith was something I left in the parking lot when I walked into the office, not because I was ashamed of it but because I genuinely believed that being professional meant compartmentalizing my beliefs. I thought integrity meant not mixing my personal convictions with my work responsibilities. (Spoiler alert: I was completely wrong, but at least I was consistently wrong.)

As I read through the Gospels with fresh eyes, I began to see Jesus's ministry through the lens of project management, and everything changed. Jesus had managed the ultimate transformation project—changing humanity's relationship with God. He had assembled a diverse team (have you ever tried managing both a tax collector and a zealot?), established clear objectives, navigated complex stakeholder relationships, and delivered results that exceeded all expectations. Most remarkably, He had done it while demonstrating principles that directly contradicted conventional management wisdom.

Think about it. Jesus had a clear mission statement (Matt. 28:19-20). He delegated responsibilities effectively and delivered the ultimate project on time, on budget, and according to specifications. He also handled scope creep like a pro. Remember when his mother tried to get him to turn water into wine before his hour had come? Classic stakeholder management.

The Transformation

In the natural realm, I was managing multiple crises simultaneously. But in the spirit realm, I was learning to navigate by faith rather than by sight, to lead by divine wisdom rather than by human understanding, and to deliver results through God's power rather than through my own ability. The wheels that had carried me through two decades of project management success were replaced by wings that could carry me through impossible circumstances.

Over the following months, I began applying biblical leadership principles to our healthcare IT program. Instead of managing through authority, I began leading through service. Instead of focusing solely on deliverables, I started prioritizing relationships. Instead of treating problems as obstacles to overcome, I began viewing them as opportunities for team growth and character development.

And do you know what happened? The project still had problems (this isn't a prosperity gospel blog, folks), but I changed. I started approaching conflicts with humility instead of defensiveness. I began viewing difficult team members as people with stories rather than obstacles to overcome.

I found myself naturally gravitating toward transparency and honesty, even when it was uncomfortable.

Most surprisingly, these weren't just feel-good changes. They actually improved project outcomes. When I stopped trying to cover up problems and started addressing them head-on, the team innovated and found effective ways to prioritize issues that could be resolved by the team or with leadership engagement, and issues to document clearly and escalate formally (and then let go and let leadership deal with it). The project team (vendor participants notwithstanding) grew closer and bonded over the experience. When I admitted I didn't have all the answers, team members stepped up with solutions I never would have discovered on my own.

Through careful scope analysis and stakeholder alignment, we successfully split the program components that were not dependent on our challenging vendor partnership. We accomplished and closed out those critical elements ahead of schedule and under budget, delivering real value to the healthcare organizations in our network. The portions of the program that remained vendor-dependent were transitioned to another capable program manager, which allowed for a clean handoff that honored both the government requirements and our professional relationships.

But the most significant change wasn't in our project outcomes; it was in my understanding of calling and purpose. I realized that God hadn't called me to be a project manager who happened to be a Christian. He had called me to be a Christian who expressed her faith through excellent project management. There's a profound difference.

The Perfect Storm That Produced Perfect Flight

Even as my personal world was falling apart, the Holy Spirit was accelerating my understanding of project management principles in ways that defied human logic. The enemy meant to destroy my calling through overwhelming circumstances, but God used those very circumstances to elevate my calling to a dimension I never knew existed.

What would have been a good book series became a powerful testimony to how biblical principles don't just work when life is easy; they work especially when you're called to soar above the storm. The insights I gained while learning to fly through crises were deeper, more profound, and more transformational than anything I had learned during comfortable seasons of wheeled success.

The Research That Changed Everything

This realization deepened during my doctoral studies in project management, even as I typed research papers with debris cleanup happening around me. As I researched leadership theory, team dynamics, and organizational change while processing personal loss, I kept finding that the most profound insights had biblical foundations. Modern management science wasn't discovering new truths; it was rediscovering ancient wisdom that Jesus had demonstrated two millennia ago.

I stumbled across research by Nelson A. Rahul that basically validated everything I'd been experiencing. His study, "The Role of Christian Values in Enhancing Efficiency and Effectiveness in Business Administration: A Project Management Perspective," was like finding out that someone had been secretly following me around, taking notes, and then publishing them in an academic journal.

Rahul's research demonstrated something that many of us have suspected but rarely seen substantiated—that Christian values don't just make you a better person, they make you a better project manager. Values such as integrity, accountability, and servant leadership aren't just nice-to-haves that make you feel warm and fuzzy; they're competitive advantages that lead to measurable improvements in project success rates.

This wasn't some fluffy, feel-good study. Rahul looked at actual project outcomes, measured efficiency metrics, and analyzed case studies where Christian principles were applied in real-world business scenarios. The results were compelling. Projects led with Christian values showed improved stakeholder satisfaction, better team cohesion, fewer legal complications, and yes, better financial performance.

This research reinforced my conviction that faith-based project management isn't about compromising professional excellence for spiritual principles. It's about discovering that biblical wisdom actually enhances our ability to deliver exceptional results while building lasting relationships and creating a meaningful impact.

Why This Book Series Matters

I discovered that when Jesus called His disciples to follow Him, He wasn't just inviting them to walk; He was preparing them to fly.

> *But those who wait on the Lord shall renew their strength; they shall mount up with wings like eagles; they shall run and not be weary, they shall walk and not faint.*
> —Isa. 40:31

We live in an era of unprecedented project complexity. Technology projects that once took years now need to be completed in months. Global teams must collaborate across time zones, cultures, and languages. Stakeholder expectations have never been higher, while project failure rates remain stubbornly high despite decades of methodology improvements.

The healthcare industry, where I've spent most of my career, desperately needs project managers who can navigate not just technical complexity but human complexity with supernatural wisdom.

We're implementing technologies that will determine whether patients receive life-saving treatments on time.

We're managing projects that directly impact whether families receive accurate diagnoses or whether elderly patients can access their medications. The stakes aren't just financial; they're literally matters of life and death.

In this environment, project management becomes ministry. Every successful implementation potentially saves lives. Every well-managed team relationship contributes to better patient care. Every project completed with excellence reflects the character of the God we serve. This isn't just about delivering technology solutions; it's about stewarding resources, developing people, and advancing God's Kingdom through our professional calling.

Traditional project management approaches, while valuable, often treat projects as mechanical processes rather than human endeavors. They focus on managing tasks rather than developing people, on controlling outcomes rather than building relationships, and on optimizing efficiency rather than creating lasting value.

Christian project managers need a different approach, one that recognizes that every project is ultimately about people serving people under the sovereignty of a loving God. We need methodologies that honor both excellence and character, that deliver results while developing relationships, that achieve earthly success while advancing eternal values.

The more I study both Scripture and project management principles, the more I realize that what we call "best practices" in the business world often echo biblical wisdom that's been around for millennia. It's almost as if the Creator of the universe might actually know something about organization, leadership, and getting things done. Go figure.

A Work of Love for Kingdom Harvest

This book series emerged from my conviction that Christian project managers need more than secular methodologies adapted with religious language. We need project management principles that are fundamentally grounded in biblical truth, tested through real-world application and spiritual warfare, and designed to honor God while delivering exceptional results.

But more than that, we need to understand that our calling as project managers isn't just about managing earthly projects; it's about learning to operate in the supernatural realm where God's Kingdom principles override natural limitations. When the wheels of human ability fall off, it's time to discover the wings of divine empowerment.

Whether you're managing a church building project, implementing a new ministry program, leading a corporate initiative, or overseeing a community development effort, you'll discover that Jesus's approach to project management offers profound wisdom for modern challenges. His principles work not because they're religious but because they reflect the fundamental truths about how humans work together most effectively—especially when facing impossible odds that require supernatural solutions.

What Faith-Based Project Management Is *Not*

Before we go further, let's establish what I'm not advocating. I'm not suggesting you start every team meeting with prayer (unless your entire team is on board with that, in which case, go for it). I'm not recommending that you quote Scripture in your status reports or replace your project charter with the Sermon on the Mount. Christian project management isn't about religious performance; it's about character-driven leadership.

This approach isn't about being preachy, ineffective, or worse, both. It's not about saying "I'll pray about it" when someone asks for your project timeline, although a little divine intervention never hurts when dealing with scope creep. And it definitely doesn't mean ending every email with "Blessings and Gantt charts."

It's about integrating timeless principles of integrity, servant leadership, stewardship, and wisdom into how you manage projects and lead teams without making your colleagues wonder if they accidentally joined a corporate prayer circle when they signed up for your project kickoff meeting.

My Foundation: Scripture and Stephen Covey

Before we dive into the content, I would like to share the primary influences that have shaped this work. First and foremost, I am a doer of the Word, not merely a hearer only. I don't just read Scripture daily; I actively seek to apply its principles in every aspect of my life and work. The Bible isn't a collection of nice stories or moral suggestions; it's the inspired Word of God that provides practical wisdom for navigating the complexities of modern life and leadership.

Every principle in this book is grounded first in Scripture, tested through real-world application, and validated through results that honor God while serving others. I approach the Bible as the ultimate management manual, written by the One who created and sustains all organizations, teams, and projects.

I must also acknowledge my deep appreciation for Stephen R. Covey's transformational works, particularly *The 7 Habits of Highly Effective People*, *The 8th Habit*, and Stephen M. Covey's book *The Speed of Trust*. Both of their principle-centered approaches to leadership resonated powerfully with my biblical worldview. Their insights on character-based effectiveness have had a profound influence on my approach to project management.

Throughout this book, you'll notice "Oh My Stephen" quotes that highlight particularly relevant insights from Stephen Covey's work. These aren't random additions. They're carefully selected principles that complement and reinforce the biblical foundations we're exploring. While Covey's principles provide valuable secular validation for biblical truths, Scripture remains the primary foundation for everything we'll discuss.

How to Use This Book

This book is designed for practicing project managers and business professionals who lead projects—those who want to integrate their faith with their professional calling. Whether you're managing church projects, corporate initiatives, community development efforts, or personal goals, you'll find principles in this book that apply directly to your situation.

Each chapter follows a consistent structure.

- **Biblical Foundation:** Every principle starts with Scripture.

- **Case Study Analysis:** Real-world examples demonstrate the principle in action.

- **Modern Application:** Practical tools and techniques apply to your current projects.

- **Personal Reflection:** Questions will help you apply the concepts to your specific situation.

Don't just read this book. Apply it. Start with one principle at a time. Test it with your current project. Observe the results. Share your experiences with other Christian professionals. Most importantly, give God the glory for the improvements you experience.

The Journey Ahead

Over the next 12 chapters, we'll explore how Jesus's approach to leadership, planning, execution, and closure provides a comprehensive framework for project management excellence. We'll discover how biblical principles address the most common project challenges such as unclear vision, dysfunctional teams, stakeholder conflicts, scope creep, resource constraints, and failure recovery.

You'll learn practical techniques like the PRAY method for risk management, the GRACE approach to conflict resolution, and the GPS principle for project navigation. More importantly, you'll discover how your project management calling can become a powerful tool for Kingdom-building and a testimony to God's faithfulness.

As you read this book, you'll encounter case studies from my own project management experience, testimonies from other Christian leaders, and practical applications you can implement immediately. You'll discover how your project management calling can become a powerful expression of your faith and a tool for advancing God's Kingdom in your workplace and community.

Faith Forward Life isn't about having all the answers; it's about asking better questions. It's about discovering that your work can be more than just a paycheck, that your projects can be more than just tasks to complete, and that your professional life can be an expression of your deepest values rather than a compromise of them.

The Master Project Manager—Jesus—is ready to teach you His methods. The question is whether you're ready to be His student. When your wheels fall off, remember that God is preparing you to fly.

Let's begin with the greatest project ever undertaken, the creation of everything that exists. In studying God's approach to this ultimate project, we'll discover foundational principles that will transform how you approach every project for the rest of your career.

I pray that the work of my hands will prosper through this labor of love and bless those who are meant to read it and share it as seeds that create good fruit crops for Kingdom harvests of souls won for heaven. May every project you manage become a testimony to the faithfulness of our God, and may every team you lead encounter the transformational power of biblical leadership principles.

Glory to God! In Jesus's name!

PART I
The Foundation of Faith-Based Leadership

Before you can lead others effectively, you must first establish the character and principles that will guide every decision. Part I explores how biblical leadership principles create the bedrock for all successful project management. Like a master builder who begins with a solid foundation, the Christian project manager must first establish servant leadership, team-building skills, and character-based authority before attempting to manage complex initiatives.

Oh My Stephen

Management is efficiency in climbing the ladder of success; leadership is determining whether the ladder is leaning against the right wall.

—Stephen R. Covey,
The 7 Habits of Highly Effective People

CHAPTER 1
The Greatest Project Ever Undertaken

In the beginning God created the heavens and the earth.

—Gen. 1:1

The Creation Project: Seven Days to Perfect Execution

Picture this: You're sitting in the executive boardroom of the universe's largest corporation, and the CEO has just announced the most ambitious project in history. The scope? Create everything that exists. The timeline? Seven days. The budget? Unlimited. The success criteria? Perfect functionality, sustainable operations, and complete stakeholder satisfaction for eternity.

Most project managers would immediately start hyperventilating into a paper bag. But God approached this ultimate project with the calm confidence of perfect planning, flawless execution, and divine project management principles that would make PMI weep with joy. The creation project wasn't just about bringing something from nothing; it was about establishing the very foundation of how successful projects should be managed.

Let's examine what we can learn from the Master Project Manager's approach to the greatest undertaking ever conceived.

Day 1: Establishing the Foundation

> *Then God said, "Let there be light"; and there was light.*
>
> —Gen. 1:3

Every seasoned project manager knows that the success of any project hinges on establishing a solid foundation from the very beginning. God didn't start with the fun stuff—creating animals or landscaping the Garden of Eden. He started with the absolute essential: light.

In our modern project management vernacular, God began with infrastructure. Before you can have deliverables, you need the basic systems that make everything else possible. Light separated day from night, thus establishing the fundamental rhythm that would govern all subsequent work. This wasn't just illumination; it was the establishment of time itself—the ultimate project management tool.

How many of us have rushed into projects without first establishing our "light"—our foundational systems, our communication protocols, our basic infrastructure? We jump straight to the exciting deliverables while skipping the unglamorous but critical groundwork. God shows us a better way: Start with what enables everything else.

The Divine Work Breakdown Structure

As we examine the creation project, we see a perfect example of logical sequencing and dependency management.

Day 1: Light (foundation/infrastructure)
Day 2: Atmosphere (environmental systems)
Day 3: Land and Vegetation (platform and initial deliverables)
Day 4: Sun, Moon, and Stars (operational systems)
Day 5: Sea and Air Creatures (primary users)
Day 6: Land Animals and Humans (stakeholders and administrators)
Day 7: Rest (project closure and celebration)

Notice how each phase builds logically on the previous one. You can't have plants without land, you can't have animals without plants, and you can't have sustainable operations without the sun and moon to govern seasons and cycles. This isn't just good project management; it's perfect project management.

Quality Control at Every Phase

And God saw that it was good.

—Gen. 1:4

After each day's work, God performed a quality review. He didn't wait until the end of the project to discover problems. He built quality assurance into every phase. The phrase "and God saw that it was good" appears seven times in Genesis 1, establishing a pattern of continuous quality monitoring that would make any Six Sigma practitioner proud.

I've seen too many projects where quality control was treated as an afterthought, scheduled for "later" when there was time. By then, defects had compounded, rework costs had skyrocketed, and stakeholder confidence had evaporated. God shows us that quality isn't something you add at the end. It's something you build in at every step.

Case Study: Noah's Ark - Managing Scope, Timeline, and Divine Requirements

Make yourself an ark of gopherwood; make rooms in the ark, and cover it inside and outside with pitch.

—Gen. 6:14

If you think your project requirements are challenging, consider Noah's situation. The project sponsor (God) had given him specifications for a vessel unlike anything ever built, with a success criteria that included saving every species on earth from a global flood that had never occurred before.

Talk about managing scope creep.

The Ultimate Stakeholder Management Challenge

Noah faced what every project manager dreads: skeptical stakeholders who questioned the very premise of the project. His neighbors, who saw him building a massive boat in the desert, thought the project was absurd from a human perspective. Yet Noah had received his requirements directly from the ultimate project sponsor.

This presents us with a crucial principle: *Faith-based project management sometimes requires moving forward when stakeholders don't understand the vision.* Noah couldn't explain the meteorological mechanics of a global flood because such a thing had never happened. He had to manage stakeholder relationships while maintaining confidence in requirements that seemed impossible.

How many times have we as Christian project managers received direction that seemed to defy conventional wisdom? Perhaps it was launching a new service line when finances were tight or implementing a technology solution that seemed overly ambitious for our organization's maturity level. Noah teaches us that sometimes obedience to clear direction is more important than consensus from skeptical stakeholders.

Precise Requirements in an Imprecise World

God's specifications for the ark were remarkably detailed.

- Length: 300 cubits
- Width: 50 cubits
- Height: 30 cubits
- Three decks with rooms throughout
- A window and door with specific placements
- Waterproofing inside and out

These weren't vague requirements like "build something that floats." They were precise specifications that Noah had to follow exactly. Yet Noah also had to exercise considerable project management judgment. How do you design room layouts for animals that vary from ants to elephants? How do you plan food storage and waste management for a floating zoo?

This balance between following explicit requirements and exercising wise judgment is something every project manager faces. We need the humility to follow clear direction precisely while having the wisdom to make good decisions in areas where we're given flexibility.

Timeline Management Under Pressure

> *For after seven more days I will cause it to rain on the earth forty days and forty nights.*
>
> — Gen. 7:4

Imagine receiving a seven-day notice that your project absolutely must be complete and operational—no extensions, no negotiating with stakeholders about delaying the flood. The ark had to be ready, stocked, and operational in seven days.

Noah's response teaches us about preparation and readiness. The text suggests that Noah had been working on this project for decades, methodically building according to specifications. When the final deadline came, he was ready, not because he crammed at the last minute but because he had been faithfully executing the project plan all along.

How many of us maintain our projects in a constant state of readiness? Too often, we operate with the assumption that we'll have time to prepare when deadlines approach. Noah shows us the wisdom of building in a margin and maintaining readiness throughout the project lifecycle.

Success Criteria: Everyone Survives

Noah's project had exactly one success metric: preserve life through the flood—not most life or important life, but all life. The ark project succeeded completely. Every species that entered the ark survived. Every human family member was preserved. The project met its requirements exactly.

That reminds us that successful projects aren't just about delivering outputs. They're about achieving outcomes. Noah didn't just build a boat; he preserved civilization and the natural world. The deliverable was the ark, but the outcome was the continuation of life itself.

Leadership Principle: "For I Know the Plans I Have for You"

"For I know the plans I have for you," says the Lord, "plans to prosper you and not to harm you, to give you hope and a future."

—Jer. 29:11

This verse, beloved by Christians worldwide, contains profound implications for how we approach project management as people of faith. It reveals three critical truths about divine project planning that should transform how we lead our earthly projects.

1. God Plans with Complete Information

When God says, "I know the plans I have for you," He's not speaking as a project manager who hopes the requirements are solid and the assumptions are valid. He's speaking as the ultimate stakeholder who has perfect knowledge of all variables, dependencies, and future states.

This should give us tremendous confidence as Christian project managers. We don't have to have perfect information to move forward faithfully. We don't need to see around every corner or predict every risk. Our role is to plan wisely with the information we have while trusting that our ultimate project sponsor has perfect knowledge of how our projects fit into God's larger plans.

I learned this lesson powerfully during a pharmacy

benefit management (PBM) implementation that defied every industry standard. Our health plan made the strategic decision not to renew our PBM contract, which gave us only six months to complete what should have been an 18-month transition to a new vendor. The decision came after discovering significant benefits to both the organization and our valued health plan members, but the timeline seemed impossible. Every consultant we hired said the same thing: PBM implementations require 12 to 18 months minimum. The regulatory requirements alone typically take eight months to navigate. Leadership was second-guessing the decision as the magnitude of the challenge became clear.

During those hectic days, I found myself praying constantly for sanity, peace, and wisdom as the pressure mounted. God answered those prayers in ways that exceeded my expectations. Stakeholders who had previously been difficult to work with suddenly began listening to my recommendations and valuing my proven skills. The synergy of our project team became unlike anything I had ever experienced. Every meeting seemed to unlock new solutions, and every challenge was met with unexpected collaboration.

I believe what happened next was truly supernatural. Divine appointments connected us with the right people at precisely the right moments. Our new PBM vendor revealed they had been developing a rapid deployment system that perfectly matched our accelerated timeline. Regulatory reviews that typically dragged on for months were expedited through processes that seemed to align perfectly with our needs. Our outgoing vendor, rather than creating obstacles, provided unprecedented cooperation during the transition. We went live in five and a half months with zero member disruptions and achieved the projected cost savings immediately. What should have been a career-ending catastrophe became a shining star in my resume portfolio. The project succeeded through divine intervention, and to this day, I give all the praise to God for making the impossible possible.

2. Plans for Prosperity, Not Harm

The Hebrew word for *prosper* in Jeremiah 29:11 is *shalom*—wholeness, completeness, well-being. God's plans aren't just about achieving deliverables; they're about creating comprehensive flourishing for all stakeholders.

That transforms how we define project success. Yes, we need to deliver on time, on budget, and according to specifications. But faith-based project management goes deeper. We're not just completing tasks; we're participating in God's work of bringing *shalom* to our organizations and communities.

When we managed the implementation of a new patient portal at our hospital, we could have defined success narrowly—system deployment, user training completion, and basic functionality testing. Instead, we expanded our success criteria to include patient satisfaction improvements, staff workflow enhancement, and reduction in administrative burden.

The result was a project that not only met its technical

requirements but genuinely improved the experience of everyone involved. Patients could access their records more easily. Nurses spent less time on documentation. Physicians had better visibility into patient compliance. The project created the kind of wholeness that reflects God's definition of prosperity.

3. Plans That Provide Hope and Future

"To give you hope and a future." This phrase from Jeremiah 29:11 captures the forward-looking nature of divine project management. God's plans aren't just about solving immediate problems; they're about building toward a better future.

As Christian project managers, we should approach every project with this same long-term perspective. How does this project contribute to the flourishing of our organization five years from now? How does it build capacity for future opportunities? How does it develop people and strengthen relationships in ways that extend far beyond the project timeline? This long-term perspective sometimes requires making decisions that seem suboptimal in the short term.

During a major website redesign project for our PMI Chapter, we had the opportunity to cut costs by using a website platform vendor known for fast implementation but with a history of poor client communication and inadequate post-launch support. The immediate budget impact would have been positive, but as vice president of communications on the board of directors, I advocated for a platform vendor that maintained transparent communication practices and provided comprehensive training and ongoing support for our volunteer team.

The project cost more up front, but the relationships we built led to better long-term website maintenance, enhanced our chapter's professional reputation in the project management community, and established a technology partnership that served us well in subsequent digital initiatives. We planned for sustainable growth and member engagement, not just immediate deliverables.

Applying Creation Principles to Modern Projects

As we close this first chapter, let's consider how the principles from the creation project apply to our work as Christian project managers.

1. **Start with Foundation, Not Features**

    Before you plan your most exciting deliverables, ensure you have the foundational systems in place. What's your "light"—the basic infrastructure that enables everything else? Don't skip the unglamorous groundwork in your eagerness to build impressive features.

2. **Build Quality into Every Phase**

    Quality isn't something you add at the end. It's something you build in at every step. Establish quality checkpoints throughout your project lifecycle, not just at final delivery.

3. **Sequence Dependencies Logically**

   God didn't create animals before plants or plants before soil. Follow the logical order of dependencies in your projects, even when stakeholders are eager to see exciting deliverables sooner.

4. **Plan for Rest and Celebration**

   God's project plan included rest. Your projects should too. Build in time for team recovery, lessons learned, and celebration of achievements.

5. **Trust Divine Timing**

   Sometimes you'll receive direction that doesn't make sense from a human perspective. Like Noah, learn to balance faithful obedience to clear requirements with wise judgment in areas of flexibility.

The creation project wasn't just about making something from nothing. It was about establishing the principles that govern all successful endeavors. As we apply these timeless truths to our modern projects, we participate in the ongoing work of bringing order from chaos, creating value from resources, and building something beautiful that serves others.

In the next chapter, we'll explore how Jesus demonstrated servant leadership principles that turn traditional project management hierarchies upside down. We'll see why leading from below might be the most effective approach for Christian project managers.

But first, take a moment to consider this: What would change about your current project if you approached it with the confidence that the ultimate project sponsor has perfect knowledge of the plans He has for you? What foundational work might you be skipping in your eagerness to build impressive deliverables? And how might building quality into every phase transform both your project outcomes and your team's experience?

The greatest project ever undertaken began with light. What light does your project need to shine before you can build everything else?

CHAPTER 2
Servant Leadership in Project Management

But Jesus called them to Himself *and said, "You know that the rulers of the Gentiles lord it over them, and those who are great exercise authority over them. Yet it shall not be so among you; but whoever desires to become great among you, let him be your servant."*

—Matt. 20:25-26

Jesus Washing the Disciples' Feet: Leading from Below

Picture the scene. It's the night before the crucifixion, and Jesus is having His final meal with the 12 men He's spent three years training to carry on His mission. These disciples have been arguing about which of them is the greatest. They're positioning themselves for leadership roles in what they assume will be Jesus's earthly kingdom. The atmosphere is thick with ambition and political maneuvering.

In any modern corporate setting, that would be the perfect moment for the CEO to deliver a rousing speech about organizational hierarchy, establish clear reporting structures, and announce who's getting promoted to which positions. Instead, Jesus does something that would make Harvard Business School professors rethink their entire curriculum.

He gets up from dinner, takes off His outer garments, wraps a towel around His waist, and begins washing His disciples' feet.

> *So when He had washed their feet, taken His garments, and sat down again, He said to them, "Do you know what I have done to you? You call Me Teacher and Lord, and you say well, for so I am. If I then, your Lord and Teacher, have washed your feet, you also ought to wash one another's feet. For I have given you an example, that you should do as I have done to you."*
>
> —John 13:12-15

This wasn't just a nice gesture or a symbolic act. Jesus was demonstrating the fundamental principle that would distinguish His followers from every other leadership philosophy—that true authority comes from service, not position.

> **Oh My Stephen**
>
> *The key to successful leadership today is influence, not authority.*
>
> —Stephen R. Covey,
> *The 7 Habits of Highly Effective People*

The Upside-Down Project Team Structure

In traditional project management, authority flows downward through clearly defined hierarchies. The project manager sits at the top of the project team structure, delegating tasks and holding team members accountable for deliverables. Commands flow down, reports flow up, and everyone knows their place in the pecking order.

Jesus turned this model completely upside down. In His organizational structure, the leader serves at the bottom of the team, supporting everyone else's success. Authority isn't about commanding others; it's about empowering them. Leadership isn't about being served; it's about serving.

That creates what I call the Inverted Authority Principle—the higher your position, the greater your responsibility to serve those under your authority. As a project manager, you don't manage people. You serve them by removing obstacles, providing resources, facilitating communication, and creating an environment where they can do their best work.

I learned this lesson the hard way during a complex technology platform implementation for the research and development department at a large biotech company early in my career. I was part of the contracted vendor team as an IT project manager and reported to our assigned senior project manager. I worked directly with our account executive leader, who became an invaluable mentor. The senior project manager took the traditional command-and-control approach, asserting authority through position and treating the client team of senior research scientists, IT administrators, and system architects as subordinates rather than partners—despite the fact that they had decades more experience and intimate knowledge of their own systems.

The results were predictably disastrous. Team meetings became tense confrontations where the senior project manager dismissed concerns, overrode technical recommendations, and publicly embarrassed team members who questioned his decisions. Critical system integration issues went unreported because people learned that bringing problems to his attention resulted in blame and frustration rather than solutions. Project quality suffered because people were more concerned with avoiding his wrath than solving complex technical challenges.

Much of my project management work became cleaning up his messes and repairing relationships he had damaged. I found myself serving as an unofficial mediator between our vendor team and increasingly frustrated client stakeholders. Through the mentoring of our account executive leader who modeled a completely different approach to client relationships, I learned to ask the client team how I could help them succeed rather than following the senior project manager's failed example of asserting authority. Instead of hoarding information like he did, I became a trusted conduit for communication, often working around him to ensure critical issues reached our account executive leader. Instead of taking credit for successful implementations, I made sure individual contributors were recognized for their technical expertise and problem-solving skills, something the senior project manager rarely did.

The transformation was remarkable. Team members began bringing problems to me before they became major roadblocks. Client stakeholders started coming directly to me for coordination needs, which allowed me to focus on obstacle removal and relationship management. Project quality improved because people felt empowered to take ownership of their technical workstreams.

Most importantly, I discovered that serving the team didn't diminish my authority. It actually enhanced it. When you're genuinely invested in others' successes, those relationships become invaluable assets that help you succeed throughout your career. Some of the relationships I developed during that project—including our account executive leader and several client stakeholders—became references for me for future jobs and promotions. The trust built through service opened doors that positional authority never could have.

Looking back, I can see the Lord's favor on me through it all, providing wisdom through mentorship and opening doors that my own abilities never could have opened. "For You, O Lord, will bless the righteous; with favor You will surround him as *with* a shield" (Ps. 5:12).

Foot-Washing Project Management

What does foot-washing look like in modern project management? It's the unglamorous work that enables others to shine.

- **Removing Obstacles:** Instead of delegating problems downward, servant leaders take on the messy work of navigating organizational politics, securing resources, and clearing bureaucratic roadblocks.

- **Providing Tools and Training:** You ensure your team has everything they need to succeed, even if it means fighting budget battles or learning new technologies yourself.

- **Taking Responsibility for Failures:** When projects go wrong, servant leaders step forward to take accountability rather than pointing fingers at team members.

- **Sharing Credit for Successes:** Recognition flows downward to the people who did the actual work, while accountability for problems flows upward to leadership.

- **Listening More Than Speaking:** In project meetings, servant leaders spend more time understanding team concerns than explaining their own vision.

This approach requires tremendous humility and security. It means celebrating others' achievements while taking responsibility for their failures. It means making your team look good even when it makes you look ordinary. It means measuring your success by their success rather than by traditional metrics like budget control or schedule adherence.

CHAPTER 3

Building Teams Like Jesus Built Disciples

Then He appointed twelve, that they might be with Him and that He might send them out to preach.

—Mark 3:14

The 12 Disciples: Diverse Skills, Unified Purpose

If Jesus had used modern recruiting practices, His team would have looked very different. Instead of fishermen, tax collectors, and political zealots, He would have assembled a group of seminary graduates with complementary skill sets, compatible personalities, and proven track records in ministry leadership. Thank goodness He didn't.

The 12 disciples represent one of history's most successful examples of building a high-performing team from unlikely components—four fishermen who probably smelled like their profession, a tax collector considered a traitor by his countrymen, a political revolutionary who wanted to overthrow the Roman government, brothers who competed for attention, a skeptic who needed proof before believing anything, and a treasurer who would eventually embezzle funds and betray the whole operation.

This wasn't a team. It was a recipe for disaster.

Yet three years later, this dysfunctional group of ordinary people had become an extraordinary team capable of launching a movement that would transform the world. How did Jesus accomplish this transformation? He did it through team-building principles that every project manager can apply today.

> **Oh My Stephen**
>
> *Synergy is better than my way or your way.*
> *It's our way.*
>
> —Stephen R. Covey,
> *The 7 Habits of Highly Effective People*

Principle 1: Recruit for Character, Train for Competence

Jesus didn't recruit based on résumés or technical skills. He recruited based on character qualities that could be developed into leadership capabilities. Peter was impulsive, but he was also courageous. Matthew was a social outcast, but he was also detail-oriented. Thomas was skeptical, but he was also thorough. John was young, but he was also passionate.

This challenges the modern approach of hiring for specific skill sets and hoping character develops over time. Jesus understood that technical skills can be taught, but character qualities are fundamental to a person's core identity. It's easier to teach a person of integrity how to manage finances than to teach a skilled accountant how to become trustworthy.

In my experience managing healthcare project teams, I've learned to prioritize character over credentials in hiring decisions. I'd rather train a person with integrity and work ethic to use new software than try to motivate a technically skilled person who lacks commitment to the mission.

Principle 2: Create Psychological Safety Before Demanding Performance

Jesus spent significant time building relationships with His disciples before giving them major responsibilities. He ate with them, traveled with them, and shared His life with them. He created an environment where they felt safe to ask questions, admit confusion, and even make mistakes.

When Peter walked on water and then began to sink, Jesus didn't use it as a teaching moment about faith failure. He simply reached out and caught him. When the disciples couldn't heal a demon-possessed boy, Jesus didn't publicly criticize their lack of faith. He quietly taught them about the power of prayer and fasting.

This psychological safety enabled the disciples to take risks, experiment with new approaches, and learn from failures without fear of rejection or punishment. It's the foundation of every high-performing team.

Principle 3: Model the Behavior You Want to See

Jesus didn't just teach servant leadership; He demonstrated it. He didn't just talk about love for enemies; He practiced it. He didn't just preach about sacrifice; He embodied it. The disciples learned more from watching Jesus than from listening to His words.

This is particularly important in project management where team members are constantly observing how leaders handle pressure, conflict, and setbacks. They notice whether you blame others when things go wrong or take responsibility. They watch how you treat difficult stakeholders and whether you practice the values you preach in team meetings. Your behavior as a project manager becomes the template for how your team members will behave under pressure.

Principle 4: Delegate with Development in Mind

After these things the Lord appointed seventy others also, and sent them two by two before His face into every city and place where He Himself was about to go.

—Luke 10:1

Jesus didn't just delegate tasks; He delegated with the specific purpose of developing His disciples' capabilities. He sent them out in pairs so they could support each other and learn from shared experiences. He gave them clear instructions but also the freedom to adapt those instructions to specific situations.

When they returned, Jesus debriefed their experiences, celebrated their successes, and helped them process their failures. This wasn't just about getting work done. It was about building people while accomplishing mission objectives.

Principle 5: Discern when to Invest and when to Replace

While Jesus invested deeply in developing His disciples, He also recognized that not everyone would respond to development efforts. Even among the 12, Judas ultimately proved unwilling to be transformed by the experience. Jesus continued to work with him until the end, but He didn't compromise the mission when it became clear that Judas would not change.

This teaches us a crucial principle. We should invest significantly in developing our team members, but we must also recognize when someone is unwilling or unable to grow into their role. Sometimes, the most loving thing to do for the individual, the team, and the mission is to help them find a better fit elsewhere.

Real-World Application: Two Tales of Development

As a program manager, I've experienced both sides of this development challenge. These contrasting experiences have taught me invaluable lessons about when to persevere and when to make difficult personnel decisions.

Success Story: From Corrective Action to Leadership

Several years ago when I was Program Manager for a large health plan initiative focused on improving the financial consumer experience for our members, I chose to have a particular Project Coordinator assigned to my program because I had worked with her before and she had provided excellent project support. But for some reason, this time was very different. Instead of the superior performance I had experienced in her previously, I encountered serious performance issues. Her work was consistently late, lacked attention to detail, and created confusion rather than clarity for the project team. I found myself working harder to fill gaps in her deliverables and reworking meeting notes and other administrative tasks that I really didn't have time for. The situation deteriorated to the point where Human Resources placed her on a corrective action plan.

My initial instinct was to replace her immediately. The program was too important, and I needed reliable project support. But something about her reaction to the corrective action plan gave me pause. Instead of making excuses or becoming defensive, she expressed genuine remorse and a sincere desire to improve. She acknowledged her shortcomings and asked for specific guidance on how to do better.

Rather than rushing to replace her, I decided to invest in her development. I created a structured coaching plan that included weekly one-on-one meetings, clear performance expectations, and regular feedback sessions. I modeled the organizational skills and communication standards I expected and gave her progressively more challenging responsibilities as she demonstrated improvement.

The transformation was gradual but remarkable. Over the following months, she not only met the requirements to get off the corrective action plan but began exceeding expectations. Her attention to detail improved dramatically, her communication became clearer and more proactive, and she started anticipating project needs rather than simply reacting to them.

By the time I left that organization a few years later, she had been promoted multiple times—from Project Coordinator to Senior Project Manager to Lead Project Manager. She had become one of the most trusted and capable project leaders in the organization. To this day, it remains one of the professional achievements I'm most proud of, not because of any project deliverable but because of the person who was developed through the process.

The Difficult Decision: When Investment Isn't Enough

In my current role as an IT Program Manager over a large, complex, government-funded technology program, I faced a similar but ultimately different situation. I had a Project

Coordinator with serious performance issues—missed deadlines, incomplete deliverables, and communication gaps that created confusion across the program.

Drawing from my previous success, I implemented the same developmental approach. I provided clear expectations, regular coaching sessions, structured feedback, and progressively challenging assignments. His attitude was excellent. He seemed genuinely appreciative of the feedback, accepted responsibility for his mistakes, and expressed enthusiasm for improvement.

But despite months of consistent effort, the performance issues persisted. Unlike my previous experience, where I saw steady improvement week by week, this situation showed no meaningful change. He continued to make the same types of errors, he still missed deadlines, and his quality of work remained below program standards.

I found myself praying regularly for wisdom about this person, asking God to either transform his capabilities or open doors for him to find a position better suited to his strengths. After extensive prayer and consultation with my leadership, I made the difficult decision to replace him with another Project Coordinator who could provide the level of support the program truly needed.

This decision was painful but necessary. Sometimes, despite our best developmental efforts, a person simply isn't a good fit for a particular role. The loving thing to do—for them, for the team, and for the mission—is to help them find a better opportunity elsewhere.

Case Study: David's Mighty Men—High-Performance Teams Under Pressure

> *Now these were the heads of the mighty men whom David had, who strengthened themselves with him in his kingdom, with all Israel, to make him king, according to the word of the Lord concerning Israel.*
>
> —1 Chron. 11:10

David's mighty men provide a fascinating case study in team development under extreme pressure. These men weren't born warriors. They were desperate outlaws who became legendary fighters through shared hardship and mutual commitment.

The Foundation: Shared Adversity

> *And everyone who was in distress, everyone who was in debt, and everyone who was discontented gathered to him. So he became captain over them. And there were about four hundred men with him.*
>
> —1 Sam. 22:2

David's team didn't start with superstars. It started with people who had nowhere else to go. They were in debt, in distress, and discontented. They came to David not because he offered them comfortable positions but because he offered them purpose and hope.

This teaches us something profound about team-building. Shared challenges can become the foundation for extraordinary unity. When people face difficulties together, they develop bonds that can't be created through team-building exercises or corporate retreats.

I've seen this principle work in challenging healthcare project implementations. Teams who struggle together through difficult go-lives, impossible deadlines, and complex technical problems often develop a camaraderie that lasts for years. They become not just colleagues but trusted friends who will support each other through future challenges.

The Process: Incremental Challenge

David didn't immediately throw his men into major battles. He started with smaller conflicts that allowed them to gradually build confidence and competence. They learned to fight together, trust each other, and develop the skills they would need for larger challenges.

This progressive development created a team that could handle increasingly complex missions. By the time they faced major enemies like the Philistines, they had already proven themselves in dozens of smaller engagements.

The Result: Legendary Performance

> *These* are *the names of the mighty men whom David had: Josheb-Basshebeth the Tachmonite, chief among the captains. He was called Adino the Eznite, because he had killed eight hundred men at one time.*
>
> —2 Sam. 23:8

The mighty men became famous for accomplishing seemingly impossible feats. Three of them broke through enemy lines just to bring David water from a well in Bethlehem. Others single-handedly defeated hundreds of enemies. They became legends, not because they were naturally gifted but because they had been developed through shared purpose and mutual support.

This kind of extraordinary performance doesn't happen by accident. It's the result of intentional team development that combines a clear mission, progressive challenge, and deep relationships.

Testimony: How Prayer Transformed My Dysfunctional Project Team

About 10 years ago, I inherited what could charitably be called a *challenging* project team. We were implementing a new bleeding-edge, consumer-driven healthcare solution nationally across all regions the organization covered, and the team dynamics were toxic. The Revenue Cycle Front-End leaders and Health Plan Finance leaders were barely speaking to each other after a disagreement about system requirements. The program director was being screamed at and belittled in steering committee meetings, and back-end users were already complaining about the system before we'd even completed the design phase.

In short, it was a project manager's nightmare. My first instinct was to address the dysfunction through traditional management approaches such as team meetings to air grievances, revised communication protocols, and clear escalation procedures for conflicts. These interventions helped somewhat, but the underlying tension remained.

That's when I decided to try something different. I prayed before and over each team meeting—not a long theological dissertation but a simple request for wisdom, unity, and success in serving our patients. I was careful to keep it inclusive and focused on our shared mission rather than on specific religious doctrine.

The change was gradual but profound. People started listening to each other more respectfully during meetings. Conflicts became discussions rather than arguments. Team members began volunteering to help each other rather than jealously guarding their own responsibilities.

The Revenue Cycle Front-End leader later told me he appreciated how I changed my approach to leading the meetings and helped him and the rest of the team remember that we were all working toward the same goal—better member experience. The Health Plan Finance leader said it reminded her that our departmental disagreements were less important than our shared mission. The developers appreciated that they felt like they were being heard and appreciated as thought partners instead of getting kicked around and wrongfully blamed for things that had nothing to do with their solution build. But the most significant change was in me. Praying for my team members by name each morning changed how I saw them. Instead of viewing them as sources of problems, I began seeing them as people with unique gifts and challenges. Instead of managing their behavior, I started serving their success.

After a very wise and timely rebaseline across scope, schedule, and budget, the project was completed on time and under budget. But more importantly, it was completed by a team that had learned to work together effectively. The solution delivered was the first of its kind in the industry. It was very well received by our health plan membership, and other healthcare organizations have since emulated it.

Lessons Learned

Prayer Changes the Pray-er: The primary beneficiary of praying for my team was me. It softened my heart toward difficult people and helped me see them as God sees them.

- *Shared Purpose Transcends Personal Conflicts:* When people remember they're working toward something bigger than themselves, petty disagreements become less important.

- *Spiritual Practices Create Emotional Safety:* Taking time to acknowledge the spiritual dimension of work helped people feel more comfortable being vulnerable and authentic with each other.

- *Small Gestures Have a Big Impact:* A thirty-second prayer at the beginning of each meeting transformed the entire team dynamic over time.

Building Teams Through Spiritual Practices

You don't have to be in a Christian organization to incorporate spiritual principles into team building. Here are some approaches that work in secular environments.

- *Start with Gratitude:* Begin meetings by acknowledging something positive that each team member has contributed.

- *Focus on Service:* Regularly remind the team how their work serves others, whether patients, customers, or the broader community.

- *Practice Forgiveness:* When conflicts arise, model the process of acknowledging hurt, accepting responsibility, and moving forward together.

- *Celebrate Character:* Recognize team members not just for technical achievements but for demonstrating integrity, courage, and compassion.

- *Create Rituals of Unity:* Develop team traditions that reinforce shared identity and purpose.

Practical Team-Building Principles for Christian Project Managers

1. The TEAM Model
   - *Trust:* Create psychological safety where people can admit mistakes and ask for help.

- *Empowerment:* Give people authority to make decisions within their areas of expertise.
- *Accountability:* Establish clear expectations and help people meet them.
- *Mission:* Keep the larger purpose visible and compelling.

2. **The Development Cycle**
   - *Recruit for Character:* Look for integrity, work ethic, and coachability.
   - *Build Relationships:* Invest time in knowing your team members personally.
   - *Provide Challenges:* Give people opportunities to grow through progressive responsibility.
   - *Celebrate Growth:* Acknowledge both individual development and team achievements.

3. **The Conflict Resolution Process**
   - *Acknowledge:* Don't ignore interpersonal problems, hoping they'll resolve themselves.
   - *Address:* Have honest conversations about issues while they're still manageable.
   - *Align:* Help conflicting parties find common ground in shared mission.

- ***Advance:*** Move forward together with renewed commitment to team success.

4. **The Legacy Perspective**
   - ***Develop Leaders:*** Your success is measured by the leaders you develop, not just the projects you complete.
   - ***Transfer Knowledge:*** Ensure that your team members can succeed without you.
   - ***Build Systems:*** Create processes that outlast your tenure on the project.
   - ***Multiply Impact:*** Prepare your team members to build great teams of their own.

Creating Your Discipleship Plan

Just as Jesus had an intentional development plan for His disciples, you should have a development plan for your team members. Here's a framework for creating individual growth plans.

Assessment Phase

- What are this person's natural strengths and abilities?
- What character qualities do they demonstrate consistently?

- What areas need development for them to reach their potential?
- What motivates them to do their best work?

Development Phase

- What experiences will help them grow in their areas of strength?
- What challenges will stretch them without overwhelming them?
- What resources and support do they need to succeed?
- How will you provide feedback and encouragement along the way?

Deployment Phase

- What responsibilities can you delegate that will utilize their strengths?
- How can you position them to lead others in their areas of expertise?
- What opportunities exist for them to advance their careers?
- How will you celebrate their growth and achievements?

Discernment Phase

- Are they responding positively to development efforts?
- Is improvement evident over a reasonable time frame?
- Do their values align with the team and organizational mission?
- If development isn't working, how can you help them find a better fit elsewhere?

The goal isn't just to complete your current project successfully. It's to develop people who will go on to lead great teams and accomplish great things for God's Kingdom. But it's also to recognize when someone needs a different opportunity to flourish, and to make those difficult decisions with wisdom and grace.

Jesus invested three years in 12 ordinary people and changed the world. He also recognized when Judas wasn't going to change and allowed him to face the consequences of his choices. Imagine what could happen if you invested your project management skills in developing the people God has placed on your team, while also having the wisdom to make difficult personnel decisions when necessary.

In the next chapter, we'll explore how biblical vision transforms project planning from a mechanical exercise into a spiritual discipline that aligns earthly work with eternal purposes.

PART II
Divine Project Planning

Even the most charismatic leader will fail without proper planning. This part of the book delves into how biblical principles transform traditional project planning methodologies. We'll discover how divine vision, providence-guided planning, and faith-based risk management create project plans that not only achieve earthly success but align with God's eternal purposes.

> **Oh My Stephen**
>
> *Begin with the end in mind.*
>
> —Stephen R. Covey,
> *The 7 Habits of Highly Effective People*

CHAPTER 4
Vision That Moves Mountains

Where there is no vision, the people perish: but he that keepeth the law, happy is he.

—Prov. 29:18 (KJV)

"Where There Is No Vision, the People Perish"

Consider what happened when C. S. Lewis first shared his vision for *The Chronicles of Narnia* in the early 1950s. He described a series of children's books that would use fantasy and allegory to explore profound spiritual truths, where talking animals and mythical creatures would help readers understand the nature of good and evil, sacrifice and redemption. His publisher was skeptical. Literary critics scoffed at the idea of a respected Oxford professor writing "fairy tales." Many assumed that children wouldn't understand the deeper meanings, while adults would dismiss the stories as too simple.

But Lewis's vision went far beyond entertainment or even education. He envisioned stories that would plant seeds of truth in young hearts, helping children develop moral imagination and preparing them to recognize divine love when they encountered it in real life. He wanted to create what he called "supposing stories"—tales that would help readers suppose what it might be like if the eternal entered the temporal.

I can personally testify to the power of Lewis's vision. *The Chronicles of Narnia* was my absolute favorite book series when I was growing up. I read all the books multiple times because I loved them so much. Each reading revealed new layers of meaning and beauty that I had missed before. Those books weren't just entertainment for me; they were formative. They shaped how I understood courage, sacrifice, redemption, and the reality that there are deeper meanings beneath the surface of everyday life. The series taught me to see beyond the immediate and temporary to glimpse the eternal truths that give meaning to our work and calling.

When *The Lion, the Witch and the Wardrobe* was published in 1950, it launched a series that has sold over 100 million copies worldwide and been translated into dozens of languages. Today, Lewis's approach to embedding profound truth in accessible narrative influences Christian communicators, educators, and artists across all mediums—including countless readers like myself who carry those stories as foundational influences throughout their lives.

Vision That Moves Mountains

That's the power of compelling vision. It transforms impossible dreams into achievable goals by mobilizing resources, inspiring innovation, and sustaining commitment through inevitable challenges. But more than that, it plants seeds that continue growing and bearing fruit in ways the original visionary could never have imagined.

But here's what made Lewis's vision particularly powerful. It wasn't just about writing successful books or building a literary reputation. It was about planting eternal truths in human hearts through stories that would outlive their author and continue teaching for generations.

Biblical vision operates on this same principle, but with eternal rather than temporal implications. It connects immediate project objectives to God's larger purposes, transforming routine work into Kingdom-building activities.

> **Oh My Stephen**
>
> *All things are created twice. There's a mental or first creation, and a physical or second creation of all things.*
>
> —Stephen R. Covey,
> *The 7 Habits of Highly Effective People*

The GPS Principle: God's Positioning System for Project Success

Modern GPS technology works by triangulating signals from multiple satellites to determine exact location and optimal routes. Similarly, biblical vision requires triangulation between three reference points: God's purposes, stakeholder needs, and available resources.

> **God's Purposes:** What is God trying to accomplish through this project? How does it serve His Kingdom and reflect His character?
>
> **Stakeholder Needs:** Who will be served by this project's success? What problems will be solved? What opportunities will be created?
>
> **Available Resources:** What gifts, talents, finances, and relationships has God provided to accomplish this work?

When these three elements align, you have more than a project plan—you have a calling. And people will follow a calling with a passion that they'll never demonstrate for mere task completion.

Case Study: Solomon's Temple – Managing Mega-Projects with Divine Vision

Now Solomon began to build the house of the Lord at Jerusalem in Mount Moriah, where the Lord *had appeared to his father David, at the place that David had prepared on the threshing floor of Ornan the Jebusite.*

—2 Chron. 3:1

Solomon's temple represents one of history's most ambitious construction projects. The scope was unprecedented—create a dwelling place for the Almighty God. The timeline was aggressive—seven years for a project that would normally take decades. The budget was enormous—equivalent to billions in today's currency. The quality standards were perfection—every detail had to honor the Creator of the universe.

Solomon completed this mega-project successfully, creating a structure so magnificent that it became the standard for architectural excellence and the symbol of God's presence among His people.

Vision Alignment: More Than Architecture

Solomon understood that he wasn't building just a building—he was creating a place where heaven and earth would meet. This vision transformed every aspect of the project, from material selection to workforce motivation.

And Solomon said: "The Lord has said He would dwell in the dark cloud. I have surely built You an exalted house, and a place for You to dwell in forever."

—1 Kings 8:12-13

The workers weren't just laying stones; they were preparing a dwelling place for God. The craftsmen weren't just carving wood; they were creating beauty that would honor the Creator. The project managers weren't just coordinating logistics; they were facilitating worship for generations to come. This vision alignment created extraordinary commitment. People worked with a precision and dedication that external motivation could never achieve. They were participating in something eternal, not just earning wages.

Resource Mobilization Through Shared Vision

Then King Solomon raised up a labor force out of all Israel; and the labor force was thirty thousand men.

—1 Kings 5:13

Solomon mobilized resources on a scale that would be impressive even today—30,000 laborers, 70,000 carriers, 80,000 stonecutters, and 3,300 supervisors. How did he convince an entire nation to contribute their best effort to a single project?

He did it through shared vision. Every Israelite understood that this temple would be their temple—a place where they and their children could worship God for generations.

It wasn't Solomon's project that required their support; it was their project that Solomon was privileged to manage.

This principle applies to modern projects as well. When stakeholders understand how project success will benefit them personally, they become partners rather than obstacles. When team members see how their work serves a larger purpose, they contribute discretionary effort that task assignments alone could never generate.

Quality Standards That Reflect the Creator

And the temple, when it was being built, was built with stone finished at the quarry, so that no hammer or chisel or *any iron tool was heard in the temple while it was being built.*

— 1 Kings 6:7

The quality standards for Solomon's temple were extraordinary. Stones were cut and fitted so precisely at the quarry that no adjustments were needed during assembly. The goal wasn't just functionality; it was perfection that would honor God.

This attention to detail reflects a fundamental principle: Our work should reflect the character of the God we serve. Shoddy work dishonors God, while excellent work brings glory to His name.

In healthcare IT projects, that means our systems should be so well-designed and thoroughly tested that they enhance rather than complicate patient care. In church building projects, it means creating spaces that facilitate worship rather than distract from it. In community development projects, it means building solutions that serve people with dignity and respect.

Sustainable Legacy Planning

So he was seven years in building it.

— 1 Kings 6:38

Solomon took seven years to build the temple, but it served as the center of Jewish worship for over 400 years. The initial investment in quality and beauty paid dividends for generations.

This long-term perspective should influence how we approach project planning. We're not just completing immediate deliverables; we're creating foundations for future growth and impact. The extra time invested in training, documentation, and relationship building will pay dividends long after the project is officially closed.

When Vision Becomes Compelling

A compelling vision has four characteristics that distinguish it from mere goal-setting.

1. **It's Bigger Than You:** Compelling visions require divine intervention to accomplish them. They're impossible through human effort alone, which creates dependence on God and unity among team members.

2. **It Serves Others:** The best visions focus on how success will benefit stakeholders rather than how it will benefit the project team. People are motivated by service more than personal advancement.

3. **It Connects to Eternity:** Biblical visions link temporal work to eternal purposes. They help people see how their daily tasks contribute to God's Kingdom.

4. **It Inspires Sacrifice:** When people truly buy into a vision, they're willing to make personal sacrifices to achieve it. They contribute discretionary effort, take ownership of problems, and persist through difficulties.

Developing Your Project Vision Statement

A biblical project vision statement should answer three questions.

1. **What is God's heart for this project?** How does this project serve God's purposes? What aspects of His character will be displayed through its success?

2. **Who will be blessed by this project's success?** What problems will be solved? What opportunities will be created? How will people's lives be improved?

3. **What will success look like?** What specific outcomes will indicate that the vision has been achieved? How will you know when the project has fulfilled its purpose?

Here's an example from a recent doctoral research project of mine studying remote to hybrid work models.

Through this research on remote to hybrid work transitions, we will honor God by seeking truth that serves organizations with wisdom, supports workers with dignity, and stewards human potential with excellence. Success will be measured not just by academic rigor and published findings, but by practical insights that help organizations create work environments where people can flourish, families can be strengthened, and communities can benefit from more flexible and sustainable employment practices.

This vision statement connected academic research to eternal values, helping team members understand how their scholarly work served a larger purpose of human flourishing.

Communicating Vision Effectively

Having a compelling vision isn't enough. You must communicate it effectively and consistently. Here are some practical strategies.

- ***Tell Stories:*** Use concrete examples of how project success will impact real people. Stories are more memorable and motivating than abstract concepts.

- ***Use Visual Aids:*** Create diagrams, mockups, or prototypes that help people visualize the end result. Visual communication is often more powerful than verbal explanation.

- ***Connect to Personal Values:*** Help team members understand how the project vision aligns with their own values and career goals.

- ***Repeat Regularly:*** Vision communication isn't a one-time event; it's an ongoing process. Reference the vision in meetings, status reports, and team communications.

- ***Celebrate Progress:*** Acknowledge milestones that demonstrate movement toward the vision. This maintains momentum and reinforces commitment.

When Vision Meets Reality

Every project faces moments when reality challenges vision. Budget constraints, timeline pressures, technical limitations, or stakeholder conflicts can make the original vision seem unrealistic or impossible. These moments test whether your vision is truly compelling or just wishful thinking.

Compelling visions survive reality checks because they're grounded in God's purposes rather than human ambition.

During a particularly challenging health plan consumer finance project, we faced a moment when technical limitations threatened to derail our vision of integrating medical services billing statements with health plan deductible balances to improve patient statement design. The easy solution would have been to reduce the scope and settle for separate, disconnected statements that would continue to confuse patients about their financial obligations.

Instead, our team innovated by wisely reducing the scope of the paper statement designs and focusing on more technically feasible and markedly better integrated digital solutions to meet our member needs. We ended up with a unified digital experience that was clearer and more helpful to patients than our original plan.

Vision doesn't eliminate problems. It provides a framework for solving problems in ways that honor God and serve others.

From Vision to Action: The Planning Bridge

Vision without action is just dreaming. Action without vision is just busy work. The bridge between vision and action is strategic planning that aligns resources with purposes.

The SMART-ER Goals Framework

Traditional project management uses SMART (Specific, Measurable, Achievable, Relevant, Time-bound) goals. Biblical project management adds two additional criteria:

- **Eternal:** How does this goal serve God's eternal purposes?
- **Relational:** How does achieving this goal strengthen relationships and serve others?

This framework ensures that project objectives contribute to both immediate success and long-term Kingdom impact.

The Three-Horizon Planning Model

- *Horizon 1:* **Immediate Deliverables (3–6 months)** – What specific outputs must be produced to demonstrate progress toward the vision?

- *Horizon 2:* **Intermediate Outcomes (6–18 months)** – What changes in behavior, systems, or relationships will indicate that the vision is being realized?

- *Horizon 3:* **Ultimate Impact (2–5 years)** – How will the world be different because this project succeeded?

This multi-horizon approach ensures that immediate actions serve long-term purposes while maintaining accountability for near-term results.

Practical Vision Development Process

Phase 1: Vision Discovery

- **Seek God's Heart:** Begin with prayer and Scripture study to understand how this project might serve God's purposes.

- **Listen to Stakeholders:** Understand the deeper needs and aspirations behind their stated requirements.

- **Assess Resources:** Inventory the gifts, talents, and opportunities God has provided for this work.

- **Research Context:** Study similar projects and organizations to understand what's possible and what pitfalls to avoid.

Phase 2: Vision Crafting

- **Draft Initial Vision:** Create a preliminary vision statement that captures the essence of what you've discovered.

- **Test with Stakeholders:** Share the draft vision with key stakeholders and gather feedback.

- **Refine and Strengthen:** Improve the vision based on feedback while maintaining its biblical foundation.

- **Finalize and Commit:** Create a final vision statement that the team and stakeholders can enthusiastically embrace.

Phase 3: Vision Communication

- **Create Multiple Formats:** Develop various ways to communicate the vision—written statements, visual presentations, stories, and testimonials.

- **Train Champions:** Equip key team members and stakeholders to communicate the vision effectively.

- **Integrate Everywhere:** Include vision references in all project communications, meetings, and documentation.

- **Monitor Understanding:** Regularly assess whether people understand and embrace the vision.

Phase 4: Vision Sustaining

- **Regular Reinforcement:** Consistently reference the vision in project activities and communications.

- **Progress Celebration:** Acknowledge milestones that demonstrate movement toward the vision.

- **Course Correction:** When project changes are needed, evaluate them against the vision to ensure alignment.

- **Legacy Planning:** Consider how the vision will be sustained after the project is completed.

Vision-Based Decision-Making

When project teams have a clear, compelling vision, decision-making becomes more straightforward. Instead of debating options based solely on technical merits or resource constraints, teams can evaluate choices based on which option best serves the vision.

The Vision Filter Process

- **Clarify the Decision:** What specifically needs to be decided, and why is this decision important?

- **Generate Options:** Brainstorm multiple approaches to addressing the decision point.

- **Apply Vision Filter:** Evaluate each option against the project vision. Which option best serves God's purposes, stakeholder needs, and effective resource use?

- **Consider Practical Constraints:** Within the vision-aligned options, which are most feasible given the timeline, budget, and capability constraints?

- **Make and Communicate:** Choose the option that best balances vision alignment with practical feasibility, and communicate the decision clearly.

When Vision Guides Difficult Choices

Vision-based decision-making is especially valuable when projects face these difficult trade-offs:

- **Quality vs. Speed:** Does the vision prioritize serving stakeholders excellently or meeting arbitrary deadlines?

- **Cost vs. Capability:** Does the vision emphasize stewardship of resources or maximizing functional capabilities?

- **Risk vs. Reward:** Does the vision encourage bold faith or prudent caution?

- **Individual vs. Team:** Does the vision prioritize individual advancement or collective success?

The vision doesn't automatically answer these questions, but it provides a framework for making choices that serve larger purposes rather than just immediate convenience.

Creating Organizational Vision Culture

Individual project visions are important, but the greatest impact comes from building organizational cultures where compelling vision is the norm rather than the exception.

Vision Leadership Development

- **Model Vision Thinking:** Consistently demonstrate how to connect immediate work to larger purposes.

- **Teach Vision Skills:** Help team members learn to develop and communicate compelling visions for their own areas of responsibility.

- **Reward Vision Alignment:** Recognize and celebrate people who make decisions that serve the organization's larger vision.

- **Share Vision Stories:** Regularly tell stories about how vision-guided decisions led to better outcomes.

Systems That Support Vision

- **Hiring Practices:** Recruit people who are motivated by purpose, not just compensation.

- **Performance Management:** Include vision alignment as a criterion for evaluating individual and team performance.

- **Strategic Planning:** Ensure organizational strategies are grounded in a compelling vision rather than just competitive analysis.

- **Communication Practices:** Create regular opportunities for vision reinforcement and refinement.

Vision is the starting point of every great project, but it's not the ending point. In the next chapter, we'll explore how biblical planning principles transform vision into executable strategies that honor God while achieving exceptional results. But first, consider these questions:

- What is God's heart for your current project? How does it serve His Kingdom purposes?

- Who will be blessed by this project's success, and how will their lives be improved?

- What would need to change about your project approach if you were guided by a compelling biblical vision?

- How might your team's motivation and performance change if they understood the eternal significance of their work?

Vision that moves mountains begins with seeing your project through God's eyes. What vision is He calling you to embrace and pursue?

CHAPTER 5
Planning with Providence

A man's heart plans his way, but *the Lord directs his steps.*

—Prov. 16:9

When Your Gantt Chart Meets God's Timeline

I used to believe that thorough planning was about controlling outcomes. If I could just identify every task, sequence every dependency, and estimate every duration with precision, then my projects would unfold exactly as designed. My Gantt charts were works of art, my risk registers were comprehensive, and my stakeholder analyses were thorough.

Then I started managing projects in the real world. That's when I discovered that the most important planning principle isn't found in any project management methodology. It's found in Proverbs 16:9. We make our plans, but God directs our steps. That doesn't mean planning is useless; it means planning is a partnership with providence. Biblical planning isn't about creating detailed road maps that leave no room for divine intervention. It's about creating flexible frameworks that honor God's sovereignty while exercising responsible stewardship of the resources He's provided.

Jesus: The Original Agile Practitioner

Before the Agile Manifesto was written in 2001, Jesus demonstrated its core principles throughout His three-year ministry. Consider how His approach embodied what we now call Agile methodology

- **Individuals and interactions over processes and tools:** Jesus prioritized relationships over rigid systems. When the Pharisees criticized Jesus's disciples for plucking grain on the Sabbath, He responded with this: "The Sabbath was made for man, not man for the Sabbath" (Mark 2:27). He valued people over processes.

- **Working software over comprehensive documentation:** Jesus focused on tangible results—healing the sick, feeding the hungry, transforming lives—rather than elaborate theological dissertations. His parables were simple, practical stories that produced immediate understanding and change.

- **Customer collaboration over contract negotiation:** Jesus continuously adapted His approach based on His audience. He spoke differently to fishermen than to Pharisees, to children than to adults, to individuals than to crowds. He was responsive to stakeholder needs rather than locked into predetermined scripts.

- **Responding to change over following a plan:** While Jesus had a clear mission (Luke 4:18-19), His methods were remarkably flexible. He canceled planned activities to address urgent needs (Mark 6:30-34), took unexpected detours to minister to individuals (John 4:4-42), and constantly adjusted His approach based on circumstances.

Jesus's Iterative Development Approach

Jesus's ministry followed what we would now recognize as Agile sprint cycles.

- **Short iterations with frequent deliverables:** Rather than waiting three years to launch His ministry, Jesus began delivering value immediately. Each town visit, each sermon, and each miracle was a working increment of the Kingdom of Heaven.

- **Continuous feedback and adaptation:** Jesus regularly gathered His team for retrospectives. "Who do people say the Son of Man is?" (Matt. 16:13 NIV) was essentially a stakeholder feedback session that led to strategic pivots in His communication approach.

- **Cross-functional teams:** Jesus's disciples came from diverse backgrounds—fishermen, tax collectors, zealots, doctors. This diversity provided multiple perspectives and capabilities for different ministry contexts.

- **Fail-fast learning:** When the disciples failed to heal the demon-possessed boy (Matt. 17:14-21), Jesus used it as a learning opportunity rather than a performance review. When they misunderstood His mission (Luke 9:54-56), He corrected the course quickly rather than abandoning the team.

> ### Oh My Stephen
>
> *The key is not to prioritize what's on your schedule, but to schedule your priorities.*
>
> —Stephen R. Covey,
> *The 7 Habits of Highly Effective People*

The Stewardship Principle of Planning

Moreover it is required in stewards that one be found faithful.

—1 Cor. 4:2

Christian project managers aren't just managing projects; they're stewarding resources that belong to God. That includes financial resources, human resources, time, and opportunities. Good stewardship requires planning that maximizes value while minimizing waste.

But stewardship goes beyond efficiency. It includes faithfulness to God's purposes, care for people's development, and attention to long-term impact. Our plans should reflect not just what we want to accomplish but how we want to accomplish it in ways that honor God.

Jesus demonstrated perfect stewardship by accomplishing the maximum eternal impact with limited earthly resources. His three-year ministry transformed the world, yet He operated with no budget, no building, and a small team of mostly uneducated followers.

The Flexibility Principle

Come now, you who say, "Today or tomorrow we will go to such and such a city, spend a year there, buy and sell, and make a profit"; whereas you do not know what will happen tomorrow. For what is your life? It is even a vapor that appears for a little time and then vanishes away. Instead you ought to say, "If the Lord wills, we shall live and do this or that."

—James 4:13-15

James doesn't criticize planning; he criticizes presumptuous planning that ignores God's sovereignty. The difference is significant. Presumptuous planning assumes we control outcomes. Faithful planning acknowledges that God may have different ideas about timing, methods, or even objectives.

This principle has profound implications for project management. Our plans should be detailed enough to guide action but flexible enough to accommodate divine redirection. We should plan as if success depends on our effort while trusting as if success depends on God's grace.

Jesus exemplified this perfectly. He had a clear product vision (establishing God's Kingdom) but remained flexible about feature implementation. When He encountered the Samaritan woman at the well, it wasn't on His project schedule, but He recognized a high-priority user story and pivoted immediately.

Case Study: Moses and the Exodus—Change Management on a National Scale

Now the sojourn of the children of Israel who lived in Egypt was four hundred and thirty years.

—Exod. 12:40

The Exodus represents history's largest change management initiative—moving two million people from slavery to freedom, from Egypt to the Promised Land, from bondage to nationhood. The scope was unprecedented, the timeline was compressed, and the stakeholder resistance was fierce.

Moses didn't have the luxury of extensive planning time. God appeared to him at the burning bush and essentially said, "Go tell Pharaoh to let My people go." There was no detailed project charter, no risk mitigation strategies, and no stakeholder analysis—just a divine mandate and a promise of God's presence.

Yet the Exodus succeeded completely. Every Israelite who wanted to leave Egypt left Egypt. The entire nation was delivered safely through the Red Sea. The most powerful empire in the world was defeated without a single military engagement.

How did Moses manage this mega-project with minimal planning time?

Principle 1: Start with Clear Direction, Not Detailed Plans

Come now, therefore, and I will send you to Pharaoh that you may bring My people, the people of Israel, out of Egypt.

—Exod. 3:10

Moses received clear direction about the objective—deliver the Israelites from Egypt—and the authority, God's backing, but he didn't receive a detailed implementation plan. He had to figure out the *how* while trusting God for the *what*.

That reflects an important principle: Clarity of direction is more important than the detail of planning. When you know where you're going and who's backing you, you can adapt your methods as circumstances change. Like Jesus, Moses operated with a clear mission but flexible tactics.

Principle 2: Plan for Resistance, Not Just Logistics

But I am sure that the king of Egypt will not let you go, no, not even by a mighty hand.

—Exod. 3:19

God warned Moses that Pharaoh would resist the change initiative. He didn't hide the difficulties or promise that the project would be easy. Instead, He prepared Moses for the reality of stakeholder opposition while assuring him of ultimate success.

Too many project managers plan for technical challenges while ignoring human resistance. They create detailed task lists while failing to address the emotional and political dimensions of change. Moses shows us that effective planning must account for the human dynamics that often determine project success or failure.

Principle 3: Expect Divine Intervention

So I will stretch out My hand and strike Egypt with all My wonders which I will do in its midst; and after that he will let you go.

—Exod. 3:20

Moses's plan included divine intervention as a key component. He wasn't just relying on human negotiation or political pressure. He was expecting God to act supernaturally on behalf of the project.

That doesn't mean Christian project managers should plan poorly and expect God to compensate for their laziness. It means we should plan thoroughly while leaving room for God to work in ways that exceed our natural capabilities. Jesus demonstrated this by planning strategically while remaining open to miraculous interventions.

Principle 4: Build in Learning Cycles

The Exodus didn't unfold according to the original timeline. What should have been an 11-day journey became a 40-year wilderness experience. From a human perspective, that looked like project failure. From God's perspective, it was necessary preparation time.

The wilderness years weren't a detour; they were a training program. The Israelites needed to learn how to function as a nation before they could successfully occupy the Promised Land. The delay wasn't a bug; it was a feature.

That teaches us that project timelines should account for learning and development time. Sometimes the most important project outcomes aren't the deliverables we planned but the capabilities we developed along the way. Jesus understood this, spending most of His time developing His disciples rather than maximizing short-term ministry output.

Principle 5: Celebrate Milestones While Maintaining Momentum

> *Then Moses and the children of Israel sang this song to the Lord, and spoke, saying: "I will sing to the Lord, for He has triumphed gloriously! The horse and its rider He has thrown into the sea!"*
>
> —Exod. 15:1

After crossing the Red Sea, Moses led the Israelites in a celebration that acknowledged God's miraculous intervention. They didn't just check "Escape from Egypt" off their task list and move on to the next milestone. They paused to recognize God's faithfulness and their own progress toward the ultimate objective.

Celebration serves multiple purposes in project management. It reinforces team morale, acknowledges progress, builds momentum for future challenges, and gives glory to God for His provision. Projects that skip celebration often lose steam before reaching their final objectives.

The TRUST-AGILE Planning Framework

Based on biblical principles, practical experience, and Jesus's Agile approach, I've developed a planning framework that balances thorough preparation with faithful dependence on God.

T - Theological Foundation

Before creating any project plan, establish the theological foundation.

- How does this project serve God's purposes?
- What biblical principles should guide our approach?
- How will we honor God through our planning and execution?
- What would Jesus prioritize in this situation?

R - Resource Assessment

Inventory the resources God has provided.

- What financial resources are available?
- What human resources and capabilities exist?
- What time constraints and opportunities exist?
- What relationships and partnerships can be leveraged?
- How can we maximize value with minimum viable resources?

U - Uncertainty Acknowledgment

Identify areas where outcomes are uncertain.

- What assumptions are we making about stakeholder behavior?

- What external factors could affect the project?
- Where might God want to redirect our efforts?
- How will we recognize and respond to divine guidance?
- What experiments can we run to reduce uncertainty?

S - *Strategic Sequencing (Agile Sprints)*

Plan in short, iterative cycles.

- What are the highest-value features to deliver first?
- What can we learn from each iteration?
- Where are the decision points that could change direction?
- How will we maintain flexibility while ensuring progress?
- What feedback loops will guide our next steps?

T - *Trust Activation*

Build trust and dependence on God into the plan.

- Where will we specifically pray for guidance?
- How will we seek wisdom from other believers?
- What practices will keep us dependent on God?

- How will we give Him glory for successes?
- How will we respond faithfully when plans change?

Jesus's Daily Agile Practices

Jesus demonstrated daily practices that modern Agile teams would recognize.

- ***Daily standups:*** Jesus regularly gathered with His disciples to align on priorities and address obstacles (Mark 6:30).

- ***User story prioritization:*** Jesus consistently prioritized the most urgent human needs over planned activities (Luke 14:1-6).

- ***Continuous integration:*** Jesus integrated lessons learned from each encounter into His ongoing ministry approach.

- ***Retrospectives:*** Jesus regularly asked questions—What do you think? Do you understand?—to assess team comprehension and adjust His teaching methods.

- ***Pair programming:*** Jesus sent disciples out in pairs (Luke 10:1) to spread knowledge and reduce risk.

Practical Planning Tools for Christian Agile Project Managers

The Providence Sprint Template

Sprint Vision: One paragraph describing what God wants to accomplish in this iteration

Success Criteria: Specific, measurable outcomes for this sprint

User Stories: Features prioritized by Kingdom value and stakeholder impact

Sprint Backlog: Detailed tasks for this iteration only

Definition of Done: Clear criteria including both functional and spiritual outcomes

Daily Questions:

- What did we accomplish for God's Kingdom yesterday?
- What will we do today to advance His purposes?
- What obstacles need divine intervention?

Sprint Review: Demonstrate working features to stakeholders and gather feedback

Sprint Retrospective: What worked well? What could improve? How did we see God working?

The Daily Agile Planning Rhythm

Morning Standup: Start each day by reviewing priorities and asking God for wisdom.

- What Kingdom work will we advance today?
- What obstacles require prayer and wisdom?
- How can we serve our teammates?

Midday Check-In: Pause to assess progress and adjust plans based on new information.

- Are we on track for today's commitments?
- What unexpected opportunities has God provided?
- Do we need to pivot based on stakeholder feedback?

Evening Retrospective: Review the day's accomplishments and lessons learned.

- What value did we deliver today?
- What did we learn about our process?
- How did we see God's guidance?

The Weekly Sprint Cycle

Monday Vision: Begin each week by reconnecting with the project vision and sprint goals.

Wednesday Wisdom: This is a mid-week retrospective to assess progress and seek guidance on challenges.

Friday Faith: End each week by demonstrating completed work and planning the next sprint.

When Plans Change: Embracing Divine Redirection

The steps of a good man are ordered by the Lord, and He delights in his way.

—Ps. 37:23

One of the most challenging aspects of biblical planning is discerning when changes are divine redirection versus human failure. Not every plan modification indicates God's intervention, but not every setback represents poor planning either.

Jesus faced this challenge when His planned retreat with the disciples was interrupted by thousands of hungry people (Mark 6:30-44). Rather than rigidly sticking to His original plan, He recognized God's redirection and pivoted to serve the immediate need. The result was the miracle of feeding the five thousand.

Here are some indicators that plan changes might reflect divine guidance.

Unexpected Opportunities: Doors open that weren't part of the original plan but clearly serve the project vision.

Resource Provision: Needed resources become available through unexpected sources.

Stakeholder Alignment: Previously resistant stakeholders become supportive of plan changes.

Peace in Uncertainty: The team experiences peace about changes even when they don't understand the reasons.

Fruit Multiplication: Modified approaches produce better results than originally planned.

A Personal Example: When God Redirected Our Patient Bill Pay Implementation

During a major healthcare IT project to deploy self-service online patient bill pay nationally across all regions our organization covered, the original plan called for a simultaneous "big bang" rollout where all regions would launch the new system over a single weekend. The plan was meticulously detailed, extensively tested in our lab environment, and approved by all stakeholders. We had invested months in development, training, and preparation across multiple time zones and regulatory environments.

Three weeks before the scheduled go-live, our testing results across the different regions revealed something we hadn't anticipated—significant variations in patient bill pay behaviors, regulatory requirements, and technical infrastructures that were regionally unique. What worked seamlessly in our Northwest pilot showed concerning error rates in the Southern California testing. The Mid-Atlantic regulatory requirements differed substantially from our Hawaii compliance framework. Each region's patient population had developed different expectations and workflows over years of localized service.

I faced a choice: Proceed with the original plan and risk widespread system failures affecting patient payments nationwide, or modify our approach based on this late-breaking intelligence.

As I prayed about the situation—spending time in prayer myself rather than just organizing team prayer sessions—I felt a growing conviction that we needed to embrace what the data was telling us. During my personal prayer time over several days, I found myself repeatedly drawn to Scripture verses about being faithful in small things before being entrusted with larger responsibilities (Luke 16:10). It became clear that trying to force a one-size-fits-all solution across diverse regional contexts wasn't honoring the unique needs of each patient population we served.

Rather than viewing this as a setback, I began to see it as divine guidance toward a more thoughtful approach. I proposed a phased regional rollout that would start with our most standardized region and gradually add complexity as we learned from each implementation. This wasn't part of our original plan, but it would allow us to maintain momentum while honoring the regional differences that could significantly impact patient satisfaction and payment processing.

The phased approach turned out to be far superior to our original plan. It allowed us to identify and resolve region-specific issues in a controlled environment before they affected our entire patient base. It provided additional training opportunities for staff in each region to become super-users before the next region launched. It built confidence and buy-in as early regional successes became proof points for more complex implementations.

What initially looked like a major setback—the discovery of significant regional variations just weeks before launch—became an opportunity for a more patient-centered and sustainable approach. The testing results that seemed to threaten our project timeline actually led us to a more successful implementation strategy—much like Jesus turning the interruption of the hungry crowd into an opportunity for miracle and ministry.

Learning to Hold Plans Lightly

Biblical Agile planning requires what I call "confident flexibility"—confidence in God's purposes combined with flexibility about methods. We plan thoroughly because we want to be good stewards, but we hold our plans lightly because we trust God's wisdom more than our own.

That doesn't mean we are wishy-washy or indecisive. It means we're committed to objectives while remaining open to alternative approaches. It means having strong convictions about why we're doing a project while maintaining humility about how it should be accomplished.

Jesus demonstrated this perfectly—unwavering commitment to His mission, complete flexibility about methods.

Planning for People, Not Just Projects

One of the biggest differences between secular and biblical planning is the emphasis on people development. Secular planning often treats people as resources to be managed. Biblical planning treats people as individuals to be developed.

Jesus exemplified this approach. His project could have been completed more efficiently without disciples. Twelve inexperienced followers certainly slowed down His immediate ministry output. But Jesus understood that developing people was part of the mission, not separate from it.

That means our project plans should include the following:

> ***Learning Objectives:*** What new skills will team members develop through this project?
>
> ***Growth Opportunities:*** How will the project stretch people beyond their current capabilities?
>
> ***Relationship Building:*** What activities will strengthen relationships within the team and with stakeholders?
>
> ***Character Development:*** How will the project create opportunities for people to demonstrate and develop character?

Legacy Planning: How will this project prepare people for greater responsibilities in the future?

The Mentoring Integration

Every project plan should include mentoring relationships that develop people while accomplishing project objectives. This might involve the following:

- Pairing experienced team members with newer ones (like Jesus with Peter)
- Creating opportunities for people to lead in their areas of strength
- Providing training that extends beyond immediate project needs
- Encouraging cross-functional collaboration that builds broader skills
- Documenting lessons learned that benefit future projects

Planning as Worship

Commit your works to the Lord, and your thoughts will be established.

—Prov. 16:3

When we approach planning as an act of worship—acknowledging God's sovereignty while exercising responsible stewardship—our planning process becomes a spiritual discipline that transforms both us and our projects.

This perspective changes how we handle planning challenges.

Resource constraints become opportunities to trust God's provision.

Timeline pressures become occasions to seek divine wisdom about priorities.

Stakeholder conflicts become chances to practice peacemaking and reconciliation.

Technical challenges become opportunities to depend on God's guidance.

Team dynamics become contexts for developing patience and servant leadership.

Planning becomes less about controlling outcomes and more about positioning ourselves to participate in what God wants to accomplish through our projects.

The Planning Prayer Process

Before Planning Sessions: Pray for wisdom, discernment, and unity among team members.

During Planning: Regularly pause to seek God's guidance on difficult decisions.

After Planning: Commit the plans to God and ask for His blessing on the work ahead.

Throughout Execution: Continuously seek God's guidance as plans are implemented and adjusted.

When Planning Meets Reality

There are many plans in a man's heart, nevertheless the Lord's counsel—that will stand.

—Prov. 19:21

The goal of biblical Agile planning isn't to create perfect plans that never change. It's to create faithful plans that honor God while serving others effectively. When reality requires plan changes, we can trust that God's purposes will prevail even when our original strategies need adjustment. That gives us the freedom to plan boldly while holding our plans humbly. We can invest significant effort in planning because planning is an act of stewardship. We can also adjust our plans gracefully because we trust God's sovereignty over outcomes.

Jesus demonstrated this perfectly. He planned strategically but pivoted gracefully when God presented better opportunities.

Practical Tips for Flexible Agile Planning

Build buffer time into all estimates: Account for the reality that estimates are uncertain and setbacks are inevitable.

Create multiple scenario plans: Develop contingency plans for different possible outcomes.

Schedule regular plan reviews: Build in formal opportunities to assess and adjust plans based on new information.

Maintain stakeholder communication: Keep stakeholders informed about plan changes and the reasoning behind them.

Document lessons learned: Capture insights that will improve future planning efforts.

Embrace the pivot: Like Jesus changing course to serve unexpected needs, be ready to adjust when God opens new doors.

Planning with providence means embracing the paradox of thorough preparation combined with humble submission to God's will. It means planning as if success depends on our effort while trusting as if success depends on God's grace.

In the next chapter, we'll explore how biblical principles transform risk management from an exercise in fear-based contingency planning into a faith-based approach that trusts God while preparing wisely for challenges.

But first, consider these reflection questions:

- How might your project planning change if you approached it as an act of worship?

- What would confident flexibility look like in your current project situation?
- How could you better integrate people development into your project plans?
- Where might God be redirecting your current project in ways you haven't considered?
- How would Jesus approach your current project challenges using Agile principles?
- What can you learn from Jesus's iterative, adaptive ministry style?

Remember, we make our plans, but God directs our steps. The question isn't whether our plans will change. It's whether we'll be faithful stewards who can adapt gracefully when they do, just as Jesus did throughout His earthly ministry.

CHAPTER 6
Risk Management Through Faith

Be anxious for nothing, but in everything by prayer and supplication, with thanksgiving, let your requests be made known to God; and the peace of God, which surpasses all understanding, will guard your hearts and minds through Christ Jesus.

—Phil. 4:6-7

The PRAY Method – Predict, Risk-Assess, Act, Yield to God

Traditional risk management is built on fear. We identify everything that could go wrong, calculate probability and impact, develop mitigation strategies, and create contingency plans. The goal is to control outcomes by anticipating and preventing problems.

This approach has value, but it often creates more anxiety than assurance. Risk registers become catalogs of catastrophic possibilities. Contingency plans multiply until they consume more resources than the actual project work. Teams become paralyzed by analysis, afraid to make decisions because every option carries potential negative consequences.

Biblical risk management takes a different approach. It acknowledges uncertainty while trusting sovereignty. It prepares wisely while depending faithfully. It identifies risks while focusing on opportunities.

The PRAY method provides a framework for biblical risk management that honors both prudent planning and faithful trust.

- **Predict:** Identify potential challenges and opportunities.
- **Risk-Assess:** Evaluate likelihood and impact using both data and wisdom.
- **Act:** Take appropriate preventive and preparatory actions.
- **Yield:** Trust God for outcomes beyond your control.

Oh My Stephen

I am not a product of my circumstances.
I am a product of my decisions.

—Stephen R. Covey,
The 7 Habits of Highly Effective People

Predict: Identifying Risks and Opportunities

Biblical risk identification goes beyond traditional project management approaches by considering spiritual and relational dimensions alongside technical and business factors.

- *Technical Risks:* What could go wrong with systems, processes, or deliverables?
- *Business Risks:* What market, financial, or organizational factors could affect success?
- *Relational Risks:* What interpersonal or communication issues could create problems?
- *Spiritual Risks:* What attitudes or actions could hinder God's blessing on the project?

The goal isn't to identify every possible risk. That's impossible and counterproductive. The goal is to identify the risks that are most likely to significantly impact project success, along with the opportunities that could accelerate achievement of project objectives.

Risk-Assess: Wisdom-Based Evaluation

Traditional risk assessment relies heavily on quantitative analysis such as probability percentages, impact ratings, and risk scores. These tools have value, but they can create false precision about inherently uncertain events.

Biblical risk assessment adds qualitative wisdom to quantitative analysis. It asks not just "How likely is this risk?"

but "What can we learn from this risk about our project approach?" It considers not just impact and probability but also spiritual and relational implications.

Quantitative Questions:

- How likely is this risk to occur?
- What would be the measurable impact on budget, schedule, or quality?
- What would mitigation cost compared to the potential impact?

Qualitative Questions:

- What does this risk reveal about our assumptions or approach?
- How would this risk affect relationships and team morale?
- What opportunities might emerge if this risk actually occurs?
- How can preparing for this risk help us serve stakeholders better?

Act: Faith-Based Response Planning

Biblical risk response goes beyond traditional mitigation strategies to include spiritual and relational actions that address root causes, not just symptoms.

- **Preventive Actions:** Steps to reduce the likelihood of negative risks
- **Preparatory Actions:** Steps to minimize impact if risks occur
- **Relational Actions:** Steps to strengthen relationships that could help navigate challenges
- **Spiritual Actions:** Steps to seek God's guidance and blessing on the project

The key is proportional response. High-impact, high-probability risks deserve significant attention and resources. Low-impact, low-probability risks may require only basic contingency planning. The goal is wise stewardship that prepares for likely challenges without becoming paralyzed by remote possibilities.

Yield: Trusting God for Ultimate Outcomes

This is where biblical risk management differs most significantly from secular approaches. After we've identified risks, assessed them wisely, and taken appropriate actions, we trust God for outcomes beyond our control.

Yielding doesn't mean being passive or irresponsible. It means recognizing that our best planning and preparation are still subject to God's sovereignty. It means holding our risk management strategies with open hands, ready to adapt when God redirects our path.

Case Study: Daniel in the Lion's Den - Managing Stakeholder Risks

> *So the governors and satraps sought to find some charge against Daniel concerning the kingdom; but they could find no charge or fault, for he was faithful; nor was there any error or fault found in him.*
>
> —Dan. 6:4

Daniel faced what modern project managers would recognize as a classic stakeholder risk—jealous colleagues who wanted to sabotage his success. As a senior administrator in the Babylonian government, Daniel had been promoted over local officials who resented his influence and effectiveness.

This stakeholder opposition wasn't just annoying; it was potentially deadly. Daniel's enemies convinced King Darius to sign a law that would make Daniel's normal religious practices punishable by death.

How did Daniel manage this extreme stakeholder risk? He managed it through principles that apply to modern project management challenges that provide a timeless template for believers facing workplace persecution.

Principle 1: Build a Reputation for Excellence

> *Then this Daniel distinguished himself above the governors and satraps, because an excellent spirit was in him; and the king gave thought to setting him over the whole realm.*
>
> —Dan. 6:3

Daniel's first line of defense against stakeholder opposition was his track record of excellent performance. His enemies had to resort to religious persecution because they couldn't find any fault with his professional work.

This teaches us that the best protection against stakeholder risks is consistent excellence in project delivery. When you consistently deliver quality results on time and within budget, you build credibility that withstands criticism. Stakeholders may disagree with your methods, but they can't argue with your results.

Principle 2: Maintain Integrity Under Pressure

> *Now when Daniel knew that the writing was signed, he went home. And in his upper room, with his windows open toward Jerusalem, he knelt down on his knees three times that day, and prayed and gave thanks before his God, as was his custom since early days.*
>
> —Dan. 6:10

When the law was passed that made Daniel's religious practices illegal, he faced a choice—compromise his convictions or accept the consequences. He chose integrity over safety, continuing his normal pattern of prayer even though he knew it would result in persecution.

Project managers face similar choices when stakeholder pressure pushes them toward compromising their values. They might be tempted to inflate progress reports, blame team members for their mistakes, or cut corners on quality to meet deadlines. Daniel shows us that maintaining integrity is more important than managing perceptions.

Principle 3: Trust God While Taking Responsibility

Cast all your anxiety on him because he cares for you.

—1 Peter 5:7

Daniel didn't try to hide his prayer life or argue his way out of the consequences. He accepted responsibility for his choices while trusting God for the outcomes. He prepared for the worst and hoped for the best.

This balance between personal responsibility and divine trust is crucial for biblical risk management. We take appropriate actions to mitigate risks while trusting God for results beyond our control.

Principle 4: Let God Vindicate Excellence

Now the king was exceedingly glad for him, and commanded that they should take Daniel up out of the den. So Daniel was taken up out of the den, and no injury whatever was found on him, because he believed in his God.

—Dan. 6:23

God's vindication of Daniel was complete. Not only was Daniel protected from the lions, but his accusers were destroyed by the same trap they had set for him. King Darius issued a decree honoring Daniel's God throughout the kingdom.

This doesn't mean that faithful project managers will always be protected from consequences of stakeholder opposition. But it does mean that God has a way of vindicating excellence and integrity over time. Our job is to do excellent work with integrity; God's job is to handle the ultimate outcomes.

When Faith Itself Becomes the Risk: A Modern Daniel Story

Blessed is the man who endures temptation; for when he has been approved, he will receive the crown of life which the Lord has promised to those who love Him.

—James 1:12

Daniel's experience isn't ancient history; it's a pattern that repeats whenever believers choose to stand firm in their convictions despite workplace pressure. Sometimes the greatest risk we face in our professional lives isn't technical failure or budget overruns. It's the risk of compromising our faith to preserve our position.

I learned this firsthand when my own commitment to biblical principles put my career directly in jeopardy. Without going into details that could compromise ongoing legal proceedings, I found myself facing a stark choice—compromise my faith to protect my livelihood or stand firm and trust God with the outcome.

The pressure was intense. I had a family to support, financial obligations to meet, and a career I had worked years to build. The safer path seemed obvious—just bend a little, stay quiet, go along to get along. But as I prayed through the situation, I kept returning to Daniel's example and Jesus's own words: "But whoever denies Me before men, him I will also deny before My Father who is in heaven" (Matt. 10:33).

Applying the PRAY Method to Faith Under Fire

Using the PRAY method, I assessed my situation much as Daniel must have assessed his.

- *Predict:* Standing firm could result in job loss, financial hardship, and career damage. But compromising could result in spiritual damage and a pattern of future compromises.

- *Risk-Assess:* The immediate financial risk was significant and measurable. The spiritual risk was eternal and immeasurable. "For what profit is it to a man if he gains the whole world, and loses his own soul?" (Matt. 16:26).

- *Act:* Like Daniel, I chose to maintain my convictions while documenting everything carefully and seeking wise counsel from mature believers and legal professionals.

- ***Yield:*** I committed the outcome to God, trusting that He would either protect my position or provide something better, just as He had done for Daniel.

What followed was a period of intense testing. I was ultimately terminated from my position under circumstances that I believe constituted religious discrimination. The financial stress was real. The uncertainty was overwhelming. But even in the midst of the trial, I began to see God's hand at work. What the enemy meant for evil, God used for good.

Within months of my termination, I found myself choosing among three job offers, each exceeding my expectations and surpassing my former position in responsibility, compensation, and workplace culture. The position I ultimately chose provided not only better opportunities but—most importantly—an environment where my faith was valued rather than viewed as a liability.

> *Now to Him who is able to do exceedingly abundantly above all that we ask or think, according to the power that works in us, to Him* be *glory in the church by Christ Jesus to all generations, forever and ever. Amen.*
>
> —Eph. 3:20-21

God didn't just restore what the enemy had stolen; He multiplied it. The lawsuit continues, but I can already see that God has vindicated my decision to trust Him rather than compromise my convictions.

When Faith Becomes the Greatest Testimony

While I was learning these lessons about faith under professional pressure, God orchestrated a divine appointment that would show me an even more powerful demonstration of biblical risk management in action. Sometimes our greatest teachers come in unexpected packages, and sometimes the most profound lessons about trusting God come from watching someone else navigate life's ultimate scope change.

During what I thought would be a routine check-in call with my coworker Lisa, she shared news that should have devastated both of us. She had been diagnosed with pancreatic cancer. Although we've never met in person—remote work keeps us states apart—I know we're kindred spirits and fellow sisters in Christ.

Here's what absolutely amazed me. The diagnosis changed nothing about her lighthearted, humorous attitude. As she told her story, the light of Christ shone so brightly through her that I felt like I needed metaphorical sunglasses. She confidently declared, "God's will be done" and expressed such joy in proclaiming God's promise that "to be absent in the body is to be present with the Lord."

I knew immediately this was one of those divine appointment situations. Lisa was acting exactly how the Word of God tells us to—with *no fear*. Her obvious victory in Christ while walking literally through the valley of the shadow of death perfectly demonstrated what many of us struggle to live out—that our attitudes and actions in the face of trials should bring glory to God and demonstrate obedience to His Word.

Managing the Ultimate Scope Change

From a project management standpoint, Lisa was facing the ultimate scope change, one that threatened to derail everything she had planned and worked toward. But instead of panic or resistance, she was responding with supernatural change management.

- She accepted the new reality without losing sight of the bigger picture.

- She maintained team morale (our entire department felt encouraged by her attitude).

- She kept her eyes on the ultimate deliverable—eternal life with Christ.

- She demonstrated grace under pressure that most of us can only aspire to achieve.

This was biblical leadership at its finest—leading from a place of trust rather than control, demonstrating faith rather than fear, and showing others what it looks like to walk by faith even when we can't see the path ahead.

The PRAY Method in Real Time

Watching Lisa navigate her diagnosis, I could see each element of the PRAY method being lived out.

- ***Predict:*** She acknowledged the reality of her situation without denial, recognizing both the medical challenges ahead and the spiritual opportunities present.

- ***Risk-Assess:*** She evaluated her circumstances from both earthly and eternal perspectives, understanding that while the physical prognosis was serious, her spiritual destiny was secure.

- ***Act:*** She chose to maintain her faith, seek appropriate medical care, and continue serving others with the same joy and dedication she had always shown.

- ***Yield:*** Her declaration of "God's will be done" demonstrated complete surrender to divine sovereignty while maintaining active faith and hope.

The Ripple Effect of Radical Faith

Lisa's testimony was already impacting our entire team. Her joy in the midst of trial was answering questions that skeptics didn't even know they had. Her peace in the face of uncertainty was demonstrating God's faithfulness in ways that no workplace praise report ever could.

This is what happens when someone chooses to trust God completely. Their faith becomes contagious, not because they're preaching or trying to convince anyone but because they're living proof that God's promises are true even in life's darkest valleys.

The contrast between my own workplace faith struggles and Lisa's supernatural response to cancer couldn't have been starker. While I had been concerned about someone's discomfort with praise reports, God was preparing me to witness faith triumph over circumstances that could destroy anyone without His strength.

Her story reminded me that sometimes the most powerful form of workplace ministry isn't about finding the right words or navigating sensitive boundaries. It's about being so anchored in Christ that others can't help but notice the difference He makes.

Lessons from the Valley

Lisa's testimony revealed several powerful truths that every Christian leader needs to understand.

> ***Faith isn't about the absence of trials; it's about God's presence in them.*** Lisa's diagnosis didn't diminish her faith; it revealed the depth of it. She was walking proof that "the Lord *is* near to those who have a broken heart, and saves such as have a contrite spirit" (Ps. 34:18).

Our response to adversity becomes our greatest leadership platform. Lisa was demonstrating something far more powerful than stakeholder confidence during project crises. She showed how spiritual authority operates when everything external seems to be falling apart.

The light shines brightest in the darkness. Lisa's joy in the face of cancer wasn't denial. It was a demonstration of Philippians 4:7, the peace that "surpasses all understanding." Her lighthearted spirit proved that our circumstances don't dictate our spiritual condition. Our relationship with Christ does.

Divine appointments often come disguised as difficult conversations. What started as a routine work call became a master class in faith under fire, reminding me what real spiritual warfare looks like.

The Legal Perspective on Faith-Based Risk Management

Applying Christian principles to project management provides an unexpected benefit—significant reduction in legal risks. When you approach contracts and vendor relationships with a commitment to honesty and fair dealing, you create clear expectations that protect everyone involved.

I've seen projects where teams took shortcuts on documentation to "move fast," only to face costly disputes later. I've witnessed organizations that played fast and loose with vendor relationships to save dollars, only to face breach of contract lawsuits that cost exponentially more.

Meanwhile, projects where I've insisted on transparent communication, meticulous documentation, and fair dealing have consistently resulted in fewer legal headaches. "Do unto others as you would have them do unto you" isn't just good theology; it's excellent risk management.

Consider how biblical principles naturally reduce legal exposure.

- ***Transparency reduces miscommunication disputes.*** Clear documentation and honest communication about challenges leave less room for misunderstandings that lead to legal conflicts.
- ***Fair dealing prevents vendor relationship breakdowns.*** When you honor contract terms, pay promptly, and treat vendors as partners rather than adversaries, they're more likely to work through difficulties rather than pursue legal remedies.
- ***Integrity builds trust that withstands pressure.*** When stakeholders know you consistently tell the truth, they're more likely to give you the benefit of the doubt during challenging situations.

The legal costs of one contract dispute can exceed an entire project budget. Biblical risk management protects against these expensive distractions by building relationships that resolve conflicts before they require legal intervention.

Common Project Risks and Biblical Responses

Technical Risk: System Failures or Integration Problems

- *Traditional Response:* Comprehensive testing, backup systems, vendor service level agreements

- *Biblical Enhancement:*
  - Pray for wisdom in technical decision-making.
  - Build vendor relationships based on mutual respect and shared objectives.
  - Plan service opportunities during problems (How we can serve stakeholders well during system downtime).
  - Document lessons learned to help future projects.

Financial Risk: Budget Overruns or Funding Shortfalls

- *Traditional Response:* Detailed cost estimates, contingency reserves, regular budget monitoring.

- *Biblical Enhancement:*
  - Seek God's guidance on financial stewardship decisions.
  - Practice radical transparency with stakeholders about financial challenges.

- Look for creative solutions that serve stakeholder needs within budget constraints.
- Trust God's provision while exercising responsible financial management.

Schedule Risk: Delays That Affect Project Timeline

- *Traditional Response:* Buffer time in schedules, critical path analysis, resource leveling
- *Biblical Enhancement:*
  - Pray for wisdom about realistic timelines that honor both stakeholder needs and team well-being.
  - Communicate honestly about delays while focusing on solutions.
  - Use delays as opportunities to improve quality or strengthen relationships.
  - Trust God's timing while working diligently toward objectives.

Team Risk: Key People Leaving or Underperforming

- *Traditional Response:* Cross-training, performance management, retention strategies
- *Biblical Enhancement:*
  - Invest in people development that serves their long-term career interests.

- Address performance issues with grace and truth.
- Create team culture that values each person's contributions.
- Trust God to provide the right people at the right time.

Stakeholder Risk: Opposition or Lack of Support

- *Traditional Response:* Stakeholder analysis, communication plans, change management
- *Biblical Enhancement:*
  - Pray for stakeholders, including those who oppose the project.
  - Seek to understand and address underlying concerns, not just surface objections.
  - Build relationships based on service rather than just project requirements.
  - Trust God to change hearts while focusing on excellent work.

The Risk Prayer Strategy

Prayer should be woven throughout every aspect of risk management, not treated as a last resort when other strategies fail.

Before Risk Assessment: Prayer for Wisdom

If any of you lacks wisdom, let him ask of God, who gives to all liberally and without reproach, and it will be given to him.

—James 1:5

Before conducting risk identification workshops, pray for wisdom to see potential challenges and opportunities that might not be obvious through traditional analysis.

During Risk Assessment: Prayer for Discernment

However, when He, the Spirit of truth, has come, He will guide you into all truth.

—John 16:13

While evaluating risks, pray for discernment to distinguish between legitimate concerns that require action and excessive worry that creates paralysis.

After Risk Response: Prayer for Protection and Guidance

The name of the Lord is a strong tower; the righteous run to it and are safe.

—Prov. 18:10

After implementing risk response strategies, pray for God's protection over the project and guidance for ongoing decision-making.

Creating Your Project Risk Prayer List

Every project should have a specific prayer strategy that addresses both identified risks and general requests for God's blessing.

- **Wisdom Prayers:** For key decisions and challenging situations
- **Protection Prayers:** For team safety and project security
- **Provision Prayers:** For necessary resources and support
- **Relationship Prayers:** For unity among team members and favor with stakeholders
- **Purpose Prayers:** For alignment with God's will and Kingdom impact
- **Persecution Prayers:** For strength and wisdom when faith is challenged

When Risks Become Reality

And we know that all things work together for good to those who love God, to those who are the called according to His purpose.

—Rom. 8:28

Despite our best risk management efforts, some risks will materialize. Systems will fail, budgets will be exceeded, key people will leave, and stakeholders will oppose our efforts. Sometimes, as in my own experience and Lisa's journey, our very faith will be challenged.

When this happens, biblical risk management provides a framework for a response that goes beyond damage control.

Immediate Response: Trust and Act

Trust God's sovereignty while taking appropriate action. This isn't fatalism; it's faith-based action that acknowledges God's control while exercising human responsibility.

Learning Response: Grow and Improve

Every materialized risk provides learning opportunities. What assumptions were incorrect? What signals were missed? How can future projects benefit from this experience? Biblical risk management treats problems as learning opportunities, not just obstacles to overcome.

Service Response: Help and Heal

When project problems affect stakeholders, focus on service and restoration. How can we minimize the impact on others? What can we do to rebuild trust and confidence? How can this setback demonstrate our commitment to serving others?

Testimony Response: Give Glory

When God helps us navigate through realized risks, give Him glory for His faithfulness. That doesn't mean ignoring human contributions, but it does mean acknowledging that our ultimate success depends on divine blessing.

> *And they overcame him by the blood of the Lamb and by the word of their testimony, and they did not love their lives to the death.*
> —Rev. 12:11

Building Risk-Resilient Teams

The best approach to risk management is building teams that can adapt quickly and respond faithfully when challenges arise. That requires the following.

- **Psychological Safety:** Environments where people feel safe reporting problems, asking for help, and admitting mistakes without fear of punishment.

- **Spiritual Foundation:** Ground team identity in relationship with God rather than project success so setbacks don't devastate people's sense of worth.

- **Learning Orientation:** Emphasize growth over blame when problems occur; treat risks as learning opportunities rather than failures to hide.

- **Service Focus:** Help teams see risk management as serving stakeholders better, not just protecting the project.

- **Faith Integration:** Regularly acknowledge dependence on God for ultimate success while taking responsibility for faithful stewardship.

Conclusion

Risk management isn't about eliminating uncertainty. It's about trusting God while preparing wisely for challenges. When we combine prudent planning with faithful trust, we can navigate any storm that threatens our projects.

The PRAY method transforms risk management from fear-based control to faith-based stewardship. But that isn't merely a project management framework; it's a Holy Spirit-guided template for actual prayer. As you face each project challenge, let the Spirit lead you to apply the following method in your conversations with God.

- **Predict** in prayer by asking God to reveal potential challenges and opportunities, guided by Scripture such as "If any of you lacks wisdom, let him ask of God" (James 1:5).

- **Risk-Assess** through prayer by seeking divine discernment, remembering that "the Spirit searches all things, yes, the deep things of God" (1 Cor. 2:10).

- **Act** in prayer by committing your plans to the Lord, knowing that "the preparations of the heart *belong* to man, but the answer of the tongue *is* from the Lord" (Prov. 16:1).

- **Yield** in prayer by surrendering outcomes to His will, declaring with Christ, "nevertheless, not as I will, but as You *will*" (Matt. 26:39).

The appropriate Scripture will vary with each situation, but the Holy Spirit will guide you to the right verses as you pray through each phase. This method helps us predict challenges and opportunities with wisdom, assess them with discernment, act with both faith and responsibility, and yield ultimate outcomes to God's sovereign will—all within the context of Spirit-led prayer.

Daniel's ancient example, my own workplace challenges, and Lisa's supernatural response to cancer all demonstrate the same truth—the greatest risks often produce the greatest rewards when we trust God through them. Whether facing political persecution, professional challenges, or life-threatening illness, the pattern remains consistent—God vindicates faithfulness and uses our trials to demonstrate His delivering power.

Lisa's lighthearted spirit in the face of such a serious diagnosis is a master class in what it means to live by faith rather than by sight. Her story reminds us that while we may navigate workplace resistance to our faith, God is always preparing divine appointments that reveal His power and love in unmistakable ways. As we continue to serve in our professional roles, let's remember that our greatest witness might not come from the words we speak in meetings but from the way we respond when life tests everything we claim to believe. Sometimes God allows valleys not to defeat us but to give us platforms from which His light can shine the brightest.

In the next chapter, we'll explore how biblical communication principles can transform project interactions from mere information exchange into heart-connecting conversations that build trust and advance Kingdom purposes.

But first, consider these reflection questions:

- How might your project's risk management change if you approached it through the PRAY method?

- What risks in your current project might actually contain hidden opportunities?

- How could prayer and spiritual practices be integrated into your risk management processes?

- What would change if you viewed risk management as a form of service to stakeholders rather than protection for the project?

- Have you ever faced a situation where maintaining your faith created professional risk? How did you respond?

Remember, we plan wisely and work diligently, but we trust God for outcomes beyond our control. This isn't passive fatalism; it's active faith that transforms how we respond to uncertainty and challenge.

Sometimes our greatest test becomes our greatest testimony when we choose to trust God rather than compromise our convictions.

PART III
Leading Through Storms

Every project faces unexpected challenges, difficult stakeholders, and moments when failure seems inevitable. This part of the book equips Christian project managers with biblical strategies for navigating the inevitable storms of project leadership. Learn how Christ-centered communication, conflict resolution, and failure recovery can transform your most challenging projects into opportunities for spiritual growth and organizational breakthrough.

> **Oh My Stephen**
>
> *Trust is the glue of life. It's the most essential ingredient in effective communication. It's the foundational principle that holds all relationships.*
>
> —Stephen M. R. Covey,
> *The Speed of Trust*

CHAPTER 7

Communication That Connects Hearts

Then He spoke many things to them in parables, saying: "Behold, a sower went out to sow."

—Matt. 13:3

When Communication Becomes Ministry

Let me start with a story that I heard secondhand but recognized it as a common happenstance in projects like it. This is a product launch communication plan so catastrophically broken that it made the confusion at the Tower of Babel seem like a masterclass in organizational alignment.

Picture this: Spring 2023, a "straightforward" mobile app redesign that should have wrapped up in three weeks. The requirements were hazier than morning fog, the success metrics shifted more frequently than a weather vane in a tornado, and the cross-functional meetings resembled support groups for people who had lost faith in coherent dialogue.

By week one, the sprint reviews had transformed into blame-shifting tournaments. By week two, the design lead was ducking the team's Slack channels like they carried some viral strain of dysfunction. By week three, they had shipped something that technically checked every box but delivered roughly zero meaningful value to their users.

But as I reflected on this scenario, wondering how I might have handled the situation if I were in the shoes of the project leader for that initiative, something unexpected happened. My thoughts drifted to the Gospel of Luke, particularly Jesus's parables, and I experienced what can only be described as a divinely inspired epiphany.

Jesus was the master facilitator, and I chided myself for not realizing it before.

Parables: The Ultimate User Stories

If Jesus had been a modern project manager, He would have revolutionized the way we write user stories. Instead of dry, technical specifications—"As a user, I want to access my account so I can view my balance"—He would have crafted compelling narratives that connected functional requirements to human hearts.

Consider the parable of the Good Samaritan. In project management terms, this is a perfect user story that defines system requirements for love and compassion—"As a traveler in need, I want help from someone who sees beyond social barriers so I can experience healing and hope regardless of my background or circumstances."

But Jesus didn't reduce this requirement to a technical specification. Instead, He told a story that revealed the heart behind the requirement. He helped His audience understand not just what needed to be done but why it mattered and how it should be done.

This is the power of parable-based communication. It connects functional requirements to human purposes in ways that inspire action, not just compliance.

> **Oh My Stephen**
>
> *Seek first to understand, then to be understood.*
>
> —Stephen R. Covey,
> *The 7 Habits of Highly Effective People*

Why Jesus Used Stories Instead of Specifications

Jesus was the master of requirements communication, but He rarely used bullet points or technical documentation. Instead, He told stories that helped people understand complex spiritual truths through familiar experiences.

The parable of the sower wasn't just about farming. It was about how people receive and respond to truth. The parable of the talents wasn't just about investing money. It was about stewardship and accountability. The parable of the prodigal son wasn't just about family dynamics. It was about God's grace and forgiveness.

Each parable served as both a functional specification and a user experience guide. People understood not just what was expected of them but how to fulfill those expectations in ways that honored God and served others.

Modern project managers can learn from this approach. Instead of communicating only what needs to be done, we should help stakeholders understand why it matters and how success will impact real people's lives.

The Heart-Connection Principle

For out of the abundance of the heart the mouth speaks.

—Matt. 12:34

Effective project communication connects hearts before it transfers information. People need to understand not just the facts about a project but the values and purposes behind those facts. They need to feel connected to the vision before they can commit to the work.

That requires a different approach to project communication.

- **Traditional Approach:** Here's what you need to do, when you need to do it, and how it will be measured.

- **Heart-Connection Approach:** Here's why this work matters, how it serves others, and what success will look like for the people we're trying to help.

The first approach generates compliance. The second generates commitment.

Case Study: Paul's Letters—Remote Team Management in the First Century

Paul, an apostle of Jesus Christ by the will of God, to the saints who are in Ephesus, and faithful in Christ Jesus: Grace to you and peace from God our Father and the Lord Jesus Christ.

—Eph. 1:1-2

The Apostle Paul managed one of history's most successful change management initiatives—establishing Christian churches throughout the Roman Empire. His "project team" was distributed across multiple time zones (before time zones existed), operated in different cultures and languages, and faced constant opposition from hostile stakeholders.

Paul couldn't rely on video conferences, project management software, or instant messaging. His primary communication tool was letters—carefully crafted messages that had to convey complex information, maintain team morale, resolve conflicts, and provide ongoing guidance for local implementation.

His letters provide a masterclass in remote team communication that modern project managers can adapt for virtual teams and distributed stakeholders.

Principle 1: Personal Connection Before Professional Content

Notice how Paul begins most of his letters—with personal greetings, expressions of gratitude, and affirmations of relationship. He didn't jump immediately into project status updates or problem-solving. He invested in relationship maintenance that created emotional safety for difficult conversations.

> *I thank my God upon every remembrance of you, always in every prayer of mine making request for you all with joy, for your fellowship in the gospel from the first day until now.*
>
> —Phil. 1:3-5

Paul understood that trust is the foundation of effective communication. Before addressing problems or making demands, he reminded people that he cared about them personally, not just professionally.

Principle 2: Context Before Content

Paul consistently provided context for his communications. He explained not just what needed to be done but why it was important and how it connected to the larger mission. He helped recipients understand how their local challenges fit into the global picture.

> *For this reason I, Paul, the prisoner of Christ Jesus for you Gentiles—if indeed you have heard of the dispensation of the grace of God which was given to me for you.*
>
> —Eph. 3:1-2

This context-setting helped recipients understand that Paul's guidance came from his broader experience and deep commitment to their success, not from arbitrary authority or personal preference.

Principle 3: Encouragement Before Correction

When Paul needed to address problems or provide corrective guidance, he typically began with encouragement and affirmation. He acknowledged what was going well before addressing what needed to change.

> *I rejoice greatly in the Lord that now at last your care for me has flourished again; though you surely did care, but you lacked opportunity.*
>
> —Phil. 4:10

This approach created emotional safety that made people more receptive to difficult messages. They knew Paul's corrections came from love and commitment to their success, not from criticism or disappointment.

Principle 4: Specific Guidance with Flexible Application

Paul provided specific guidance for common challenges while acknowledging that local teams would need to adapt his recommendations to their unique situations. He gave principles rather than rigid rules.

> *Be anxious for nothing, but in everything by prayer and supplication, with thanksgiving, let your requests be made known to God.*
>
> —Phil. 4:6

This guidance was specific enough to be actionable but flexible enough to be applicable across different cultures and circumstances.

Principle 5: Future Focus with Present Application

Paul consistently connected immediate actions to long-term vision. He helped people understand how their current work contributed to eternal purposes, which motivated persistence through temporary difficulties.

> *Therefore, my beloved brethren, be steadfast, immovable, always abounding in the work of the Lord, knowing that your labor is not in vain in the Lord.*
>
> —1 Cor. 15:58

This future focus provided motivation that transcended immediate challenges and setbacks.

Testimony: How Heart-Centered Communication Transformed My Dysfunctional Consumer Healthcare Team

Do you remember the personal testimony I shared in Chapter 3, "How Prayer Transformed My Dysfunctional Project Team"? Let me reframe it to show how I applied the communication principles we've been exploring.

The consumer-driven healthcare solution project wasn't just a team-building challenge; it was a masterclass in what happens when communication breaks down and how biblical communication principles can restore it. The Revenue Cycle Front-End leaders and Health Plan Finance leaders weren't just having disagreements about system requirements; they had stopped truly listening to each other. The toxic dynamics, the screaming in steering committee meetings, the premature complaints about a system we hadn't even finished designing—all of them stemmed from a fundamental communication failure.

Looking back, I can see that I initially approached the dysfunction with traditional project management thinking—manage behavior, establish protocols, create escalation procedures. I was treating the symptoms of poor communication rather than addressing the root cause: people didn't feel heard, understood, or valued.

The transformation began when I shifted from information-transfer communication to heart-connection communication. That simple prayer before each meeting wasn't just a spiritual practice; it was the first step in honoring the people in the room. But prayer without genuine listening is just wishful thinking.

Applying the HEART Communication Model

The real breakthrough came when I stopped trying to communicate *to* people and started communicating *with* them. After that pivotal stakeholder meeting where the chief medical officer said, "You ask for our feedback, but you don't really understand what we're afraid of losing," I realized I needed to apply what Jesus modeled in His parables—connect functional requirements to human hearts.

- *Honor the Person:* Instead of viewing resistance as defiance, I began recognizing it as evidence that people cared deeply about their work and their patients. When Revenue Cycle leaders pushed back on pricing transparency, I started seeing someone passionate about maintaining quality care rather than someone being difficult.

- *Empathize with Their Experience:* I spent that afternoon visiting each stakeholder group with one simple question: "What are you most worried about with this consumer-driven healthcare approach?" This wasn't just active listening; it was seeking to understand the project from their perspective before explaining it from mine, exactly as Paul modeled in his letters.

- ***Align with Their Values:*** What I discovered through empathetic listening was profound. Revenue Cycle leaders weren't opposing transparency; they were protecting the doctor-patient relationship from commoditization. Finance leaders weren't being obstructionist; they were safeguarding partnerships that ensured network stability. Everyone shared the same core values: better patient outcomes, sustainable healthcare economics, and professional integrity. They just couldn't see how our disruptive platform would preserve and advance those values.

- ***Respond to Their Needs:*** Instead of generic status updates, I began providing information that specifically addressed each group's deepest concerns. For Revenue Cycle leaders, I showed how controlled transparency could actually strengthen provider-patient relationships by building trust. For Finance leaders, I demonstrated how phased rollouts could enhance rather than undermine partnership negotiations. I was practicing Paul's principle of providing specific guidance with flexible application.

- ***Trust Through Transparency:*** Following Paul's model of encouragement before correction, I started sharing both our successes and struggles openly. When we encountered technical challenges, I explained them honestly while maintaining confidence in our solutions. When stakeholder feedback led to scope changes, I communicated the reasoning transparently rather than imposing decisions from authority.

The Communication Transformation

Applying the HEART communication principles consistently produced three key changes that Christian project managers can expect to see.

1. **People began asking collaborative questions instead of defensive ones.** Instead of "Why is this taking so long?" stakeholders started asking, "What obstacles are you facing, and how can we help?" This shift indicated that people were beginning to see each other as partners rather than adversaries.

2. **My own listening fundamentally changed.** Prayer didn't just soften my heart; it transformed how I heard stakeholder concerns. Complaints became windows into people's values and priorities. When someone expressed frustration,

I heard passion for what they were protecting rather than an obstruction to overcome.

3. **Heart-centered communication became contagious.** Without any prompting from me, stakeholders began practicing these principles with each other. The Finance leader started acknowledging patient care concerns before discussing the pricing strategy. Developers began explaining technical constraints in terms of user experience impact.

The result was meetings that people looked forward to rather than dreaded and voluntary collaboration that extended beyond required project checkpoints.

Connecting to Biblical Communication Principles

This experience taught me that Jesus's parable-based communication wasn't just about spiritual truth; it was about connecting functional requirements to human hearts. When I stopped delivering technical specifications and started telling stories about how our platform would help real patients navigate healthcare more effectively, stakeholders began seeing the vision rather than just the disruption.

Paul's remote team management principles proved equally powerful. His practice of personal connection before professional content transformed how I opened every meeting. His context-before-content approach helped stakeholders understand how their local concerns fit into our broader transformation mission. His encouragement-before-correction method made people more receptive to necessary changes.

Lessons for Project Communication

Heart Connection Precedes Mind Alignment: Until people feel understood and valued, they can't fully engage with new ideas. Technical excellence means nothing without relational trust.

Resistance Reveals Values: Instead of viewing pushback as opposition, I learned to see it as valuable information about what people care most deeply about preserving—exactly what Jesus uncovered through His patient, story-based approach.

Prayer Changes the Pray-er: The primary beneficiary of praying for my team was me. It softened my heart toward difficult people and helped me see them through God's eyes—as beloved individuals with legitimate concerns rather than obstacles to overcome.

Small Spiritual Practices Have a Large Impact: A thirty-second prayer combined with genuine empathetic listening transformed our entire team dynamic over time, proving that biblical communication principles work even in secular environments.

Shared Purpose Transcends Personal Conflicts:
Once people remembered they were working toward something bigger than their departmental interests—better healthcare for real patients—petty disagreements became manageable differences of opinion.

This experience convinced me that the most sophisticated project management methodologies are useless if people don't trust each other enough to communicate honestly. But when you apply biblical communication principles—leading with your heart while engaging their minds—even the most dysfunctional teams can accomplish extraordinary things together.

The HEART Communication Model

Based on biblical principles and practical experience, I've developed a communication framework that prioritizes heart connection alongside information transfer.

H – Honor the Person

Begin every communication interaction by acknowledging the value and dignity of the people you're addressing. This might involve the following:

- Recognizing their expertise and contributions
- Acknowledging the challenges they're facing

- Expressing gratitude for their involvement in the project
- Treating their concerns as legitimate and important

E – *Empathize with Their Experience*

Seek to understand the project from their perspective before explaining it from yours. This involves the following:

- Asking questions about their concerns and priorities
- Listening for emotions behind their words
- Acknowledging the impact that project changes will have on their work
- Validating their feelings even when you can't change the circumstances

A – *Align with Their Values*

Connect project objectives to values and priorities that matter to your audience. This might include the following:

- Explaining how the project serves patients, customers, or other stakeholders they care about
- Showing how project success will help them achieve their professional goals

Communication That Connects Hearts

- Demonstrating how the project reflects the organizational values they embrace
- Linking project activities to larger purposes that they find meaningful

R – Respond to Their Needs

Provide information and solutions that address their specific needs and concerns. This involves the following:

- Giving them the information they need to do their jobs effectively
- Offering support and resources that help them succeed
- Adapting your communication style to their preferences and learning styles
- Following up to ensure their needs are being met

T – Trust Through Transparency

Build trust by being honest about challenges while maintaining confidence about solutions. This includes the following:

- Sharing both good news and bad news in a timely manner
- Acknowledging what you don't know while committing to find answers

- Explaining the reasoning behind decisions that affect them
- Following through on commitments and communicating about any changes

Practical Communication Tools for Project Managers

The Story-Based Status Report

Instead of traditional bullet-point status reports, try narrative formats that help stakeholders understand progress in human terms.

> This week, our new patient portal helped Mrs. Johnson access her lab results from home, allowing her to discuss them with her family before her follow-up appointment. This represents the kind of improved patient experience we're working to create across all our services.

The Concern-Solution Format

When addressing problems or changes, use a format that acknowledges concerns before presenting solutions.

> I understand that the new workflow will require additional training time when you're already busy with patient care. Here's how we're planning to make that training as efficient and convenient as possible.

The Vision-Connection Technique

Regularly connect immediate tasks to long-term vision using bridge statements.

I know this testing phase feels tedious, and here's why it's worth the extra effort: every bug we catch now is a problem that won't affect patient care later.

The Feedback Loop Process

Create structured opportunities for two-way communication.

- **Ask Specific Questions:** "What's working well with the new process? What's creating problems?"

- **Listen for Themes:** Look for patterns in feedback that indicate systemic issues.

- **Respond with Action:** Show that feedback leads to concrete improvements.

- **Close the Loop:** Follow up to confirm that actions addressed the original concerns.

Advanced Communication Strategies

The Parable Approach for Complex Concepts

When explaining complex technical concepts, use familiar analogies that help people understand.

Think of our new security system like the locks on your house. The firewall is like your front door lock— it keeps obvious intruders out. Multi-factor authentication is like your deadbolt—it provides an extra layer of protection. And our monitoring system is like a security alarm that alerts us if someone tries to break in.

The Stakeholder Journey Mapping

Map out the emotional journey that different stakeholder groups will experience during your project.

- **Phase 1: Awareness:** How will they first learn about the project? What will their initial reaction be?
- **Phase 2: Understanding:** What information do they need to understand why the project matters?
- **Phase 3: Engagement:** How will they become actively involved in project success?
- **Phase 4: Adoption:** What support do they need to successfully use project deliverables?
- **Phase 5: Advocacy:** How can they become champions who help others succeed?

The Multi-Channel Communication Strategy

Different people prefer different communication methods. Create multiple channels that serve different preferences.

- **Visual Learners:** Diagrams, flowcharts, infographics, and demonstration videos

- **Auditory Learners:** Verbal presentations, recorded explanations, and discussion sessions
- **Kinesthetic Learners:** Hands-on training, interactive demonstrations, and pilot programs
- **Reading/Writing Learners:** Written documentation, detailed emails, and structured reports

The Cultural Communication Adaptation

In diverse organizations, adapt your communication style to different cultural preferences.

- **High-Context Cultures:** Provide more background information and relationship context.
- **Low-Context Cultures:** Be direct and specific about requirements and expectations.
- **Hierarchical Cultures:** Ensure proper respect for authority and decision-making processes.
- **Egalitarian Cultures:** Emphasize collaboration and shared decision-making.

When Communication Gets Difficult

A soft answer turns away wrath, But a harsh word stirs up anger.

—Prov. 15:1

Every project includes difficult conversations—budget overruns, schedule delays, scope changes, performance issues, and stakeholder conflicts. Biblical communication principles are especially important during these challenging interactions.

The Gentle Truth Approach

When delivering difficult news, combine honesty with gentleness.

- **Acknowledge the Impact:** "I know this delay will affect your department's planning."
- **Take Responsibility:** "Here's what we could have done differently."
- **Focus on Solutions:** "Here's how we're working to minimize the impact."
- **Commit to Communication:** "I'll keep you updated as we make progress."

The Restoration Process

When communication breaks down or conflicts occur, practice this:

- **Own Your Part:** Acknowledge how you contributed to the problem.
- **Seek Understanding:** Try to understand the other person's perspective.
- **Find Common Ground:** Identify shared objectives and values.

Communication That Connects Hearts

- **Rebuild Together:** Collaborate on solutions that serve everyone's interests.

The Escalation Prevention Strategy

Most communication problems can be prevented through proactive relationship management.

- **Regular Check-ins:** Schedule brief but frequent conversations with key stakeholders.
- **Early Warning Systems:** Create mechanisms for people to raise concerns before they become crises.
- **Relationship Investments:** Spend time building personal connections outside of project work.
- **Trust Banking:** Consistently deliver on small commitments to build credibility for larger requests.

Building Communication Culture

Individual communication skills are important, but the greatest impact comes from building organizational cultures where excellent communication is the norm.

Communication Leadership Development

- **Model Excellence:** Consistently demonstrate clear, honest, and caring communication.

- **Teach Skills:** Help team members develop their own communication capabilities.
- **Reward Quality:** Recognize and celebrate people who communicate effectively.
- **Share Stories:** Tell stories about how good communication led to better project outcomes.

Systems That Support Communication

- **Regular Rhythms:** Establish predictable patterns for status updates, feedback sessions, and stakeholder check-ins.
- **Multiple Channels:** Provide various ways for people to share information and concerns.
- **Documentation Standards:** Create templates and guidelines that make communication more effective.
- **Feedback Mechanisms:** Build in formal and informal ways for people to improve their communication.

Communication Metrics and Improvement

- **Stakeholder Satisfaction:** Regularly measure how well people feel informed and heard.
- **Message Clarity:** Test whether key messages are being understood as intended.

- **Response Timeliness:** Track how quickly important communications are answered.
- **Relationship Health:** Assess the quality of working relationships across the project team.

The Spiritual Dimension of Communication

Let your speech always be *with grace, seasoned with salt, that you may know how you ought to answer each one.*

—Col. 4:6

For Christian project managers, communication is more than a professional skill. It's a spiritual discipline that reflects God's character and advances His Kingdom.

Communication as Ministry

Every conversation is an opportunity to do the following:

- Demonstrate God's love through genuine care for others.
- Practice biblical virtues like patience, kindness, and humility.
- Build relationships that strengthen the body of Christ.
- Serve others by helping them understand and succeed.

Prayer and Communication

- **Before Difficult Conversations:** Pray for wisdom, patience, and the right words.
- **During Conflicts:** Silently ask for God's guidance while listening and responding.
- **After Misunderstandings:** Pray for reconciliation and better communication in the future.
- **For Your Team:** Regularly pray for team members by name, asking God to bless their work and relationships.

Communication That Bears Fruit

By this My Father is glorified, that you bear much fruit; so you will be My disciples.

—John 15:8

Excellent communication in project management should produce spiritual fruit.

- **Love:** Building genuine care and concern among team members
- **Joy:** Creating positive working relationships that people enjoy
- **Peace:** Resolving conflicts in ways that strengthen rather than divide

- **Patience:** Demonstrating grace when communication is difficult
- **Kindness:** Treating all stakeholders with dignity and respect
- **Goodness:** Using communication to serve others rather than advance personal agendas
- **Faithfulness:** Being reliable and trustworthy in all communications
- **Gentleness:** Speaking truth in ways that build up rather than tear down
- **Self-Control:** Managing emotions and responses appropriately

Biblical communication transforms projects from task-focused exercises into relationship-building opportunities that create lasting value beyond project deliverables.

In the next chapter, we'll explore how to handle conflicts that inevitably arise in complex projects, using Jesus's approach to turn disagreements into opportunities for greater unity and understanding.

But first, consider these reflection questions:

- How might your project communication change if you focused first on connecting hearts rather than transferring information?
- What stories could you tell that would help stakeholders understand why your project matters?

- Which stakeholders in your current project most need to feel heard and understood?
- How could you apply the HEART communication model in your next difficult conversation?

Remember, people don't resist projects. They resist feeling unheard, unvalued, or uninformed. When we communicate in ways that honor their dignity and address their concerns, resistance transforms into partnership.

CHAPTER 8
Conflict Resolution the Jesus Way

Blessed are the peacemakers, for they shall be called sons of God.

—Matt. 5:9

The GRACE Method: Gentle, Respectful, Authentic, Compassionate, Empowering

Conflict is inevitable in project management. When you bring together diverse people with different priorities, perspectives, and personalities to accomplish challenging objectives under pressure, disagreements will occur. The question isn't whether conflicts will arise; it's how you'll handle them when they do.

Traditional project management treats conflict as a problem to be solved quickly so work can continue. Biblical project management treats conflict as an opportunity to build stronger relationships and create better solutions through collaborative problem-solving. Jesus encountered constant conflict during His earthly ministry. Religious leaders challenged His authority. Disciples argued about their relative importance. Crowds demanded different things from His mission. Yet He consistently transformed conflict into opportunities for teaching, growth, and deeper understanding.

The GRACE method provides a biblical framework for handling project conflicts in ways that honor God while advancing project objectives.

- **Gentle:** Approach conflicts with humility and kindness.

- **Respectful:** Honor the dignity and perspective of all parties.

- **Authentic:** Be honest about problems while maintaining hope for solutions.

- **Compassionate:** Seek to understand and address underlying needs.

- **Empowering:** Help all parties contribute to solutions.

Stephen R. Covey wrote, "When you really listen to another person from their point of view, and reflect back to them that understanding, it's like giving them emotional oxygen."

The Root Causes of Project Conflict

Most project conflicts stem from a few common sources that can be addressed proactively.

- **Unclear Expectations:** When people have different understandings of roles, responsibilities, or deliverables

- **Resource Competition:** When multiple priorities compete for limited time, money, or people

- **Communication Breakdown:** When information isn't shared effectively or consistently

- **Value Conflicts:** When people have fundamentally different beliefs about what's important

- **Personality Clashes:** When different working styles or communication preferences create friction

- **External Pressures:** When outside forces create stress that affects team dynamics

- **Pride and Defensiveness:** When ego prevents us from admitting mistakes or hearing correction

Understanding these root causes helps project managers address conflicts at their source rather than just managing symptoms.

Using Resistance as Diagnostic Data

One of the most counterintuitive aspects of Jesus's leadership was how He handled team pushback. Rather than viewing resistance as disloyalty or obstruction, He consistently used it as valuable information about what needed to be addressed.

Even at the Great Commission—the final "all-hands meeting"—Matthew records, "When they saw Him, they worshiped Him; but some doubted" (Matt. 28:17). This wasn't a failure of leadership development; it was realistic acknowledgment that even committed team members will have legitimate concerns about major changes.

Jesus's response reveals a crucial principle: Resistance often contains important data about Jesus's response, which reveals a crucial principle: Resistance often contains important data about implementation gaps, unclear communication, or unaddressed concerns. Instead of dismissing doubts, wise leaders investigate what those doubts reveal about the change process.

The Three Types of Productive Resistance

1. **Process Pushback:** Questions about how change will be implemented

2. **Values Pushback:** Concerns about whether changes align with the organizational mission

3. **Capacity Pushback:** Worries about whether adequate support and resources exist

Each type of resistance provides valuable diagnostic information that can strengthen the final approach. When team members raise concerns about project direction or implementation, consider these questions:

- What legitimate concerns might be driving their resistance?
- What information gaps might exist that are creating uncertainty?
- What past experiences might be influencing their current reactions?
- What additional support or clarification might help address their concerns?

By treating resistance as data rather than defiance, project managers can often transform potential conflicts into collaborative problem-solving opportunities.

Gentle: The Power of Soft Strength

Take My yoke upon you and learn from Me, for I am gentle and lowly in heart, and you will find rest for your souls.

—Matt. 11:29

Gentleness doesn't mean weakness. It means strength under control. When Jesus cleansed the temple, He was firm about what needed to change, but He was also purposeful and measured in His response. He didn't lose control or attack people personally. He addressed the behavior that was dishonoring God. In project conflicts, gentleness means the following:

- Addressing issues directly but without personal attacks
- Using calm, measured tones even when discussing serious problems
- Focusing on behaviors and outcomes rather than character flaws
- Creating emotional safety that allows honest dialogue
- Maintaining respect for all parties even during disagreements
- Approaching our own mistakes with humility rather than defensiveness

Gentle approaches often accomplish more than aggressive ones because they reduce defensiveness and create openness to change.

Respectful: Honoring Dignity in Disagreement

> Be *kindly affectionate to one another with brotherly love, in honor giving preference to one another.*
> —Rom. 12:10

Respect means treating all parties as valuable people with legitimate perspectives, even when you disagree with their positions. That doesn't mean all perspectives are equally valid, but it does mean all people deserve dignity and consideration.

In project contexts, respect involves the following:

- Listening to understand, not just to respond
- Acknowledging valid points even when you disagree with conclusions
- Avoiding public embarrassment or humiliation
- Giving people opportunities to save face while changing positions
- Recognizing expertise and contributions even during conflicts
- Honoring others when they correct our mistakes

Authentic: Truth with Love

But, speaking the truth in love, may grow up in all things into Him who is the head—Christ.

—Eph. 4:15

Authenticity means being honest about problems while maintaining hope for solutions. It means addressing real issues rather than avoiding them, but doing so in ways that build relationships rather than damage them.

Authentic conflict resolution involves the following:

- Naming problems clearly without exaggerating their impact
- Taking responsibility for your own contributions to conflicts
- Sharing your perspective honestly while remaining open to other viewpoints
- Expressing emotions appropriately without being controlled by them
- Focusing on solutions rather than dwelling on problems
- Admitting when you're wrong without making excuses

The Humility Factor: When Pride Meets Project Plans

Sometimes the most important aspect of authentic conflict resolution is the hardest—admitting when we're wrong. Pride can transform minor misunderstandings into major relationship breakdowns, while humility can turn our mistakes into opportunities for deeper trust. "He who covers his sins will not prosper, But whoever confesses and forsakes *them* will have mercy" (Prov. 28:13).

You know that sinking feeling when you realize you've been adamantly mistaken about something important? I experienced it in full HD clarity during a government healthcare project when our vendor's project manager politely but firmly corrected our team's understanding of a critical milestone.

After initially wanting to double-down on our position (because, let's be honest, admitting you're wrong in front of government stakeholders feels about as comfortable as wearing a hair shirt), I had to rebuke my pride and face the truth that we were wrong, and they were right.

Before crafting my apology email, I gathered my team for what turned out to be one of the most humbling meetings of my career. When I walked in, still wanting to argue our case, one of my senior team members lovingly but firmly said, "Let's look at this objectively. What exactly was said, and what do we actually have documented?" As we reviewed our notes together, it became painfully clear that our recollection was off. That moment of wise counsel from my team—their willingness to speak truth in love—prevented me from compounding our error with stubborn pride.

The Gift of Wise Counsel

> *Open rebuke* is *better than love carefully concealed. Faithful* are *the wounds of a friend, but the kisses of an enemy* are *deceitful.*
>
> —Prov. 27:5-6

My team's willingness to lovingly correct my initial impulse to argue was exactly the kind of faithful wound I needed. They demonstrated that sometimes the most loving thing we can do for our leaders is to help them see clearly when pride is clouding their judgment.

> *Without counsel, plans go awry, but in the multitude of counselors they are established.*
> —Prov. 15:22

That team meeting wasn't just about reviewing facts. It was about seeking collective wisdom to ensure we responded with integrity rather than defensiveness.

Bearing Good Fruit in Professional Relationships

What struck me most about this experience was how it provided an opportunity to demonstrate the fruit of the Spirit that Paul describes in Galatians 5:22-23. Love meant putting the project's success and our working relationship above my ego. Kindness required crafting an apology that honored the vendor's professionalism rather than making excuses. Gentleness showed in how I approached the correction—not defensively, but with humility. Self-control was crucial in that moment when I wanted to argue our position instead of acknowledging the truth. And faithfulness meant following through on our commitment to implement better communication protocols.

The peace that followed our reconciliation was tangible. You could feel the tension dissolve and trust begin to rebuild. Sometimes the joy of project management comes not from being right but from making things right.

Practical Steps for Humble Conflict Resolution

When you realize you've made a mistake that's causing conflict, here's your biblical project management recovery plan:

1. **Seek Wise Counsel First:** Don't craft your response in isolation. Gather your trusted team members and review the facts objectively. Be open to loving correction.

2. **Stop and Assess Quickly:** Don't let pride marinate. "Pride *goes* before destruction, and a haughty spirit before a fall" (Prov. 16:18).

3. **Own It Completely:** Take full responsibility without deflecting to team members, unclear requirements, or communication challenges.

4. **Apologize Specifically:** Address exactly what you got wrong, not just that misunderstandings happened.

5. **Acknowledge Their Correctness:** Give credit where it's due and recognize their professionalism.

6. **Implement Preventive Measures:** Show you're serious about not repeating the mistake.

7. **Focus Forward:** After apologizing, shift to solution mode and collaborative next steps.

The Unexpected Blessing

Here's what surprised me. The vendor project manager's response was not only gracious and appreciative, but he shared something remarkable. Without knowing about me writing this book at the time or the "Oh My Stephen" quotes, he told me how this reminded him of a previous boss who had a direct connection to Stephen R. Covey. Like me, he admired and was influenced by Covey's books.

As Covey wisely observed, "We judge ourselves by our intentions and others by their behavior." In that moment of humble confession, I had the opportunity to show my true intentions rather than defend my faulty behavior. Our relationship is actually stronger now than before the mistake. It turns out that humility paired with the fruit of the Spirit is a pretty effective project management tool.

This divine appointment—where a mistake became a bridge to deeper understanding through our shared appreciation for Covey's wisdom—convinced me to incorporate the story into this very chapter you're reading now. Sometimes God uses our failures to create connections we never could have planned.

Maybe that's why Jesus taught us to pray, "And forgive us our debts, as we forgive our debtors" (Matt. 6:12). In the kingdom of project management, as in the Kingdom of Heaven, grace has a way of turning our failures into foundations for better relationships.

Compassionate: Understanding Underlying Needs

But when He saw the multitudes, He was moved with compassion for them, because they were weary and scattered, like sheep having no shepherd.

—Matt. 9:36

Compassion means seeking to understand and address the underlying needs that drive conflicting positions. People rarely fight about what they say they're fighting about. They fight about deeper needs for recognition, security, control, or belonging.

Compassionate project managers look beyond surface disagreements to answer these questions:

- What fears or concerns are driving resistant behavior?
- What needs are not being met that create frustration?
- What values are being threatened that create defensive reactions?
- What past experiences are influencing current responses?
- What outcomes would help all parties feel successful?

Empowering: Creating Collaborative Solutions

But Jesus, being aware of it, said to them, "Why do you reason because you have no bread? Do you not yet perceive nor understand? Is your heart still hardened?"

—Mark 8:17

Rather than just telling people what to do, Jesus often asked questions that helped them discover answers for themselves. This empowering approach creates ownership and commitment that imposed solutions rarely achieve.

Empowering conflict resolution helps all parties do the following:

- Identify their own interests and priorities
- Generate creative solutions that serve multiple needs
- Take ownership of implementation steps
- Build skills for handling future conflicts independently
- Maintain dignity and self-respect throughout the process

Case Study: The Council at Jerusalem–Resolving Doctrinal Disputes

And certain men *came down from Judea and taught the brethren, "Unless you are circumcised according to the custom of Moses, you cannot be saved." Therefore, when Paul and Barnabas had no small dissension and dispute with them, they determined that Paul and Barnabas and certain others of them should go up to Jerusalem, to the apostles and elders, about this question.*

—Acts 15:1-2

The Jerusalem Council faced what modern organizations would recognize as a fundamental policy dispute. The question was whether Gentile converts to Christianity needed to follow Jewish law, particularly circumcision, to be considered true believers. This wasn't just a theological disagreement; it was a conflict that threatened to split the early church. Different factions had strong convictions based on their understanding of Scripture, their cultural backgrounds, and their experience with God's work among different people groups.

How did the apostles handle this potentially explosive conflict? They handled it through a process that demonstrates biblical conflict resolution principles that modern project managers can apply.

Principle 1: Acknowledge the Legitimacy of the Conflict

The apostles didn't minimize the disagreement or rush to a quick decision. They recognized that this was a significant issue that deserved careful consideration and broad input from church leaders. "Now the apostles and elders came together to consider this matter" (Acts 15:6). In project management, that means taking conflicts seriously rather than dismissing them as personality clashes or communication problems. When people have strong disagreements, there are usually legitimate underlying issues that need to be addressed.

Principle 2: Create a Safe Forum for Discussion

The Jerusalem Council created a structured environment where all parties could present their perspectives without interruption or immediate contradiction. That allowed for full understanding of different viewpoints before moving to decision-making. "And when there had been much dispute, Peter rose up *and* said to them" (Acts 15:7). Notice that they allowed "much dispute" before moving to resolution. That wasn't seen as a problem to be eliminated quickly but as a necessary part of reaching a good decision.

Principle 3: Ground Discussion in Shared Values

Peter, Paul, and James all referenced their shared commitment to God's will and the evidence of His work among different people groups. They moved the discussion from personal preferences to shared principles. "But we believe that through the grace of the Lord Jesus Christ we shall be saved in the same manner as they" (Acts 15:11). In project conflicts, that means identifying shared objectives and values that all parties care about and then using those as the foundation for finding solutions.

Principle 4: Listen to Experience and Evidence

The Council listened carefully to testimonies about what God was actually doing among the Gentiles, not just what they thought should happen based on their theological theories.

"Then all the multitude kept silent and listened to Barnabas and Paul declaring how many miracles and wonders God had worked through them among the Gentiles" (Acts 15:12). Project managers should similarly focus on evidence and results, not just opinions and preferences. What does the data show? What have we learned from experience? What approaches have actually worked in similar situations?

Principle 5: Seek Win-Win Solutions

Rather than having one side win and the other lose, the Jerusalem Council found a solution that honored both the concerns of Jewish believers and the freedom of Gentile converts.

"Therefore I judge that we should not trouble those from among the Gentiles who are turning to God, but that we write to them to abstain from things polluted by idols, *from* sexual immorality, *from* things strangled, and *from* blood" (Acts 15:19-20). This solution maintained the essential spiritual requirements while removing cultural barriers that would have made conversion unnecessarily difficult for Gentiles.

Principle 6: Communicate Decisions Clearly

The Jerusalem Council didn't just make a decision; it communicated it clearly with reasoning that helped everyone understand the rationale behind the conclusion. "For it seemed good to the Holy Spirit, and to us, to lay upon you no greater burden than these necessary things" (Acts 15:28). This communication approach acknowledged divine guidance while also taking human responsibility for the decision.

Real-World Application: Resolving a Budget Conflict

A healthcare IT project was facing a budget shortfall due to unexpected infrastructure requirements that were discovered during system testing. The clinical team wanted to proceed with full implementation, arguing that patient safety required the complete system. The finance team wanted to reduce the scope significantly to stay within budget. The executive team was caught between competing priorities and pressures.

Traditional approaches would have involved executive decision-making that left one side disappointed. Instead, I used the GRACE method to find a solution that served everyone's underlying needs.

Gentle Approach

Instead of immediately scheduling a budget meeting to "resolve" the conflict, I spent time with each stakeholder group to understand their perspectives and concerns. I acknowledged the legitimacy of each position and avoided taking sides in the initial discussions.

Respectful Listening

I discovered that the clinical team's push for full implementation was driven by concerns about patient safety during the transition period. The finance team's push for scope reduction was driven by concerns about fiscal responsibility and organizational sustainability. Both concerns were valid and important.

Authentic Communication

I shared the full financial reality with all stakeholders, including the clinical team, while also sharing the patient safety concerns with the finance team. This transparency helped everyone understand the full scope of the challenge.

Compassionate Understanding

Through deeper conversations, I learned that the clinical team would accept a phased implementation if they could be assured that patient safety wouldn't be compromised during the transition. The finance team would support additional funding if they could see a clear plan for staying within overall organizational budget constraints.

Empowering Collaboration

Rather than presenting solutions, I facilitated sessions where all parties could collaborate on creative approaches. That led to a phased implementation plan that addressed patient safety concerns while spreading costs across multiple budget cycles.

The Outcome

The final solution satisfied everyone's core needs.

- **Clinical Team:** Patient safety was protected through careful sequencing of implementations.
- **Finance Team:** Budget constraints were respected through multi-year planning.
- **Executive Team:** Organizational goals were achieved without creating lasting conflict among departments.
- **Project Team:** We had clear direction and stakeholder support for moving forward.

More importantly, the process strengthened relationships among departments and created a model for handling future conflicts collaboratively.

The Seven Steps of Biblical Conflict Resolution

Based on Matthew 18:15-17 and other biblical principles, here's a systematic approach to handling project conflicts.

Step 1: Self-Examination

And why do you look at the speck in your brother's eye, but do not consider the plank in your own eye?

—Matt. 7:3

Before addressing conflicts with others, examine your own contributions to the problem. What assumptions might you be making? How might your communication style be contributing to misunderstandings? What biases might be affecting your perspective? Are you being defensive about something you got wrong?

Step 2: Direct Conversation

Moreover if your brother sins against you, go and tell him his fault between you and him alone.

—Matt. 18:15

Address conflicts directly with the people involved rather than talking about them with others. That prevents gossip and gives people opportunities to resolve issues at the lowest possible level. Sometimes the conversation involves admitting your own mistakes first.

Step 3: Facilitated Discussion

But if he will not hear, take with you one or two more, that "by the mouth of two or three witnesses every word may be established."

—Matt. 18:16

If direct conversation doesn't resolve the conflict, involve a neutral third party who can facilitate discussion and help ensure all perspectives are heard fairly.

Step 4: Organizational Intervention

And if he refuses to hear them, tell it to the church.

—Matt. 18:17

If facilitated discussion doesn't work, involve appropriate organizational leadership that has the authority to make binding decisions about the conflict.

Step 5: Acceptance or Separation

But if he refuses even to hear the church, let him be to you like a heathen and a tax collector.

—Matt. 18:17

In extreme cases where people refuse to participate in good-faith conflict resolution, it may be necessary to limit their involvement in the project or organization.

Step 6: Forgiveness and Restoration

Then Peter came to Him and said, "Lord, how often shall my brother sin against me, and I forgive him? Up to seven times?" Jesus said to him, "I do not say to you, up to seven times, but up to seventy times seven."

—Matt. 18:21-22

The goal is always restoration and reconciliation, not punishment or exclusion. When people acknowledge their mistakes and commit to change, forgiveness should be immediate and complete.

Step 7: Learning and Prevention

> *Now all these things happened to them as examples, and they were written for our admonition.*
>
> —1 Cor. 10:11

After resolving conflicts, capture lessons learned that can help prevent similar problems in future projects. What systemic issues contributed to the conflict? What processes or communications could be improved?

The Fruit of the Spirit in Conflict Resolution

When we handle conflicts biblically, we have opportunities to demonstrate the fruit of the Spirit described in Galatians 5:22-23.

- *Love* means putting the project's success and working relationships above our ego.
- *Joy* sometimes comes not from being right but from making things right.
- *Peace* follows reconciliation and creates an environment where others can extend grace.

- *Long-suffering* shows patience with others' defensive reactions and willingness to work through difficulties.

- *Kindness* requires crafting responses that honor others' professionalism rather than making excuses.

- *Goodness* means actively pursuing what's right and beneficial for all parties.

- *Faithfulness* involves following through on commitments to implement better communication.

- *Gentleness* shows in how we approach corrections—not defensively but with humility.

- *Self-control* is crucial when we want to argue our position instead of acknowledging the truth.

Creating a Conflict-Resistant Project Culture

The best approach to conflict resolution is conflict prevention through intentional culture building.

Clear Expectations

- Define roles and responsibilities precisely.
- Establish communication protocols and decision-making processes.

- Create shared understanding of project objectives and success criteria.
- Document agreements to prevent future misunderstandings.

Psychological Safety

- Create environments where people feel safe expressing concerns.
- Encourage questions and feedback without fear of retribution.
- Model vulnerability by acknowledging your own mistakes and limitations.
- Celebrate learning from failures rather than hiding them.

Regular Check-Ins

- Schedule regular one-on-one meetings with team members.
- Use retrospectives to identify and address emerging issues.
- Create anonymous feedback mechanisms for sensitive concerns.
- Monitor team dynamics and address problems early.

Values Alignment

- Regularly discuss and reinforce shared values.
- Connect project work to larger purposes that inspire commitment.
- Recognize and celebrate behavior that demonstrates organizational values.
- Address behavior that contradicts stated values quickly and directly.

The Spiritual Dimension of Conflict Resolution

If it is possible, as much as depends on you, live peaceably with all men.

—Rom. 12:18

For Christian project managers, conflict resolution is more than a management skill. It's a spiritual discipline that reflects God's character and advances His Kingdom.

Conflict as Ministry Opportunity

Every conflict provides opportunities to do the following:

- Demonstrate Christ's love through patient, gracious responses.
- Practice biblical virtues like humility, forgiveness, and peacemaking.

- Build bridges between people who might otherwise remain divided.
- Create testimonies of God's power to restore relationships.

Prayer in Conflict Resolution

- *Before Addressing Conflicts:* Pray for wisdom, patience, and the right approach.
- *During Difficult Conversations:* Silently ask for God's guidance and peace.
- *After Misunderstandings:* Pray for healing and restoration of relationships.
- *For Opposing Parties:* Pray for those who create conflict, asking God to bless them.

The Fruit of Peacemaking

Now the fruit of righteousness is sown in peace by those who make peace.
—James 3:18

Biblical conflict resolution should produce spiritual fruit.

- *Stronger Relationships:* Conflicts resolved well often result in deeper trust and understanding.
- *Character Growth:* Working through difficulties develops patience, humility, and wisdom.

- *Organizational Health:* Healthy conflict resolution creates cultures of trust and collaboration.
- *Kingdom Witness:* How we handle disagreements demonstrates God's love to watching colleagues.

When Conflicts Can't Be Resolved

And if he refuses to hear them, tell it to the church. But if he refuses even to hear the church, let him be to you like a heathen and a tax collector.

—Matt. 18:17

Sometimes, despite best efforts, conflicts cannot be resolved because one or more parties refuse to participate in good-faith problem-solving. Here's what you can do in those situations.

- *Protect the Project:* Take necessary steps to prevent unresolved conflict from derailing project objectives.
- *Protect Relationships:* Minimize damage to other team relationships and organizational culture.
- *Protect Your Character:* Maintain integrity and biblical values even when others don't.
- *Learn and Improve:* Capture lessons that will help prevent similar situations in the future.

The goal is never to "win" conflicts but to restore relationships and advance shared objectives. When that's not possible, we can still respond in ways that honor God and serve others well.

Conclusion

Conflict is not the enemy of successful projects; unresolved conflict is. When handled biblically, conflicts become opportunities to build stronger teams, create better solutions, and demonstrate God's love in practical ways.

The GRACE method, grounded in humility and guided by the fruit of the Spirit, transforms our approach to conflict from mere problem-solving to relationship-building and character development. Sometimes the path to resolution requires us to humble ourselves, admit our mistakes, and trust that grace has the power to turn our failures into foundations for better relationships.

Remember the words of Jesus: "Blessed *are* the peacemakers, for they shall be called sons of God" (Matt. 5:9). Your role in resolving conflicts isn't just about project success; it's about reflecting God's character in a world that desperately needs more peacemakers.

Consider these reflection questions:

- How might your approach to conflict change if you viewed it as an opportunity for ministry rather than just a problem to solve?

- Which element of the GRACE method do you find most challenging to implement?

- What current conflict in your project might benefit from the seven-step biblical resolution process?

- How could you help create a more conflict-resistant culture in your organization?

- When was the last time you had to humble yourself and admit a mistake in a professional setting? How did it affect the relationship?

CHAPTER 9

When Projects Fail: Redemption and Restoration

And the Lord said to Simon, "Simon, Simon! Indeed, Satan has asked for you, that he may sift you *as wheat. But I have prayed for you, that your faith should not fail; and when you have returned to* Me, *strengthen your brethren."*

—Luke 22:31-32

Peter's Denial and Restoration: Second Chances in Leadership

Project failure is every project manager's nightmare. Despite careful planning, dedicated effort, and the best intentions, some projects simply don't achieve their objectives. Systems fail, budgets are exceeded, timelines are missed, and stakeholders lose confidence. In these moments, it's tempting to focus on blame assignment, damage control, and career preservation. But failure doesn't have to be the end of the story.

Peter's denial of Jesus represents one of history's most dramatic leadership failures. After three years of training, after declaring his willingness to die for Jesus, after promising that he would never abandon his leader, Peter denied even knowing Jesus when the pressure became intense.

By any measure, this was a catastrophic failure. Peter had abandoned his mission, betrayed his leader, and destroyed his credibility as a spokesperson for the movement. In modern terms, he had failed so completely that his project management career should have been over.

But Jesus had a different perspective on failure and restoration.

> *So when they had eaten breakfast, Jesus said to Simon Peter, "Simon, son of Jonah, do you love Me more than these?" He said to Him, "Yes, Lord; You know that I love You." He said to him, "Feed My lambs."*
>
> —John 21:15

Three times Jesus asked Peter about his love, giving him three opportunities to reaffirm his commitment—once for each denial. Then Jesus reinstated Peter to leadership with the command to "feed My lambs." The failure wasn't ignored, but it also wasn't final. Peter was restored to greater responsibility than he had before his failure.

This pattern of failure, restoration, and greater service provides a biblical framework for handling project failures in ways that honor God while building stronger leaders and organizations.

The Redemptive Purpose of Failure

> *And we know that all things work together for good to those who love God, to those who are the called according to* His *purpose.*
>
> —Rom. 8:28

Biblical perspective on failure differs fundamentally from secular approaches. Secular thinking treats failure as waste—lost time, money, and opportunities that should have been avoided. Biblical thinking treats failure as raw material for growth, learning, and character development.

That doesn't mean we should be careless with resources or casual about project outcomes. It means that when failures occur despite our best efforts, we can trust God to bring good from difficult circumstances.

The key is learning to distinguish between failures that result from poor stewardship (which require repentance and changed behavior) and failures that result from circumstances beyond our control (which require trust and perseverance).

Learning from Failure Without Being Defined by It

Peter's restoration demonstrates how to process failure in healthy ways.

- **Acknowledge Reality:** Peter didn't minimize his failure or make excuses. He acknowledged that he had denied Jesus and accepted responsibility for his actions.
- **Accept Forgiveness:** When Jesus offered restoration, Peter received it rather than continuing to punish himself for his mistakes.
- **Apply Lessons:** Peter's later leadership reflected lessons learned from his failure. He became more humble, more dependent on God, and more compassionate toward others' weaknesses.
- **Advance the Mission:** Peter didn't let his past failure paralyze his future service. He accepted greater responsibility and used his experience to strengthen others.

Grace vs. Being a Pushover: The Leadership Balance

One of the most challenging aspects of applying biblical principles to project management is understanding the difference between extending Christian grace and becoming a pushover. Peter's restoration story provides crucial insights into this balance.

The Grace Jesus Showed Peter

Jesus demonstrated several key elements of biblical grace in restoring Peter.

- **Accountability with Love:** Jesus didn't ignore Peter's failure or pretend it didn't matter. He addressed it directly but without condemnation.

- **Restoration with Responsibility:** Jesus restored Peter to leadership but with clear expectations and accountability measures.

- **Forgiveness with Boundaries:** Jesus forgave Peter completely, but that didn't mean there were no consequences or lessons to be learned.

- **Trust with Verification:** Jesus trusted Peter with future responsibility while also providing ongoing guidance and correction.

When Grace Becomes Enabling

Christian project managers sometimes confuse grace with avoiding difficult conversations or failing to hold people accountable. That misunderstanding can lead to the following:

- **Repeated Poor Performance:** Accepting substandard work in the name of "grace" while team members never improve.

- **Boundary Violations:** Allowing team members to consistently miss deadlines or ignore project standards.
- **Resource Waste:** Failing to address inefficiencies or poor stewardship because confrontation seems "unloving."
- **Team Demoralization:** When poor performers aren't addressed, high performers become frustrated and disengaged.

Biblical Boundaries in Project Management

The Bible provides clear guidance on maintaining appropriate boundaries while extending grace.

If your brother or sister sins, go and point out their fault, just between the two of you. If they listen to you, you have won them over.

—Matt. 18:15 (NIV)

Brothers and sisters, if someone is caught in a sin, you who live by the Spirit should restore that person gently. But watch yourselves, or you also may be tempted.

—Gal. 6:1 (NIV)

Biblical grace includes the following:

- **Clear Expectations:** Setting and communicating standards that honor God and serve stakeholders effectively

When Projects Fail: Redemption and Restoration

- **Consistent Accountability:** Following through on consequences when standards aren't met, while maintaining respect for the person
- **Opportunity for Growth:** Providing training, mentoring, and support to help people improve
- **Progressive Responses:** Escalating interventions when initial grace-filled approaches don't produce change
- **Protection of Others:** Ensuring that one person's poor performance doesn't harm the entire team or project.

Practical Application: The Restoration Framework

When team members fail or underperform, use this biblical framework.

Step 1: Private Conversation

- Address the issue directly but privately.
- Focus on behavior and impact, not character.
- Listen to understand circumstances and obstacles.
- Offer support and resources for improvement.

Step 2: Clear Expectations

- Establish specific, measurable improvement goals.
- Set reasonable timelines for change.

- Provide necessary training or resources.
- Document agreements and expectations.

Step 3: Ongoing Support

- Check in regularly to monitor progress.
- Celebrate improvements and growth.
- Address obstacles as they arise.
- Maintain encouragement while holding standards.

Step 4: Escalation If Necessary

- If improvement doesn't occur, involve HR or senior leadership.
- Consider role adjustments that better fit the person's capabilities.
- Make difficult decisions about team composition when necessary.
- Maintain dignity and respect throughout the process.

The Humility-Boundaries Balance

True biblical humility doesn't mean being a doormat. Consider these principles:

- **Humility *with* Strength:** Acknowledge your own limitations and mistakes while still maintaining project standards and team accountability.

- **Gentleness *with* Firmness:** Address issues with kindness and respect while being clear about expectations and consequences.

- **Patience *with* Progress:** Allow time for growth and improvement while ensuring that project objectives and team morale aren't compromised.

- **Forgiveness *with* Learning:** Extend forgiveness readily while ensuring that lessons are learned and changes are made.

Case Study: The Tower of Babel–When Pride Derails Projects

And they said, "Come, let us build ourselves a city, and a tower whose top is *in the heavens; let us make a name for ourselves, lest we be scattered abroad over the face of the whole earth."*

—Gen. 11:4

The Tower of Babel represents one of history's most spectacular project failures. The scope was ambitious—build a tower that reaches to heaven. The team was unified—"Now the whole earth had one language and one speech" (Gen. 11:1). The resources appeared adequate—advanced construction techniques and abundant materials. Yet the project failed completely, resulting in the scattering of the people and the confusion of languages.

What went wrong? The project failed not because of technical limitations or resource constraints but because of flawed motivation and misaligned purpose.

The Root Cause: Pride-Driven Objectives

The builders of the Tower of Babel weren't trying to serve God or help others. They were trying to make a name for themselves. Their motivation was self-glorification rather than stewardship. They wanted to build something impressive that would establish their reputation and prevent their dispersion.

That pride-driven approach contained the seeds of its own destruction. When our projects are motivated primarily by personal advancement, organizational ego, or competitive advantage rather than service to others, they become vulnerable to failure that accomplishes God's humbling purposes.

The Warning Signs of Pride-Driven Projects

Modern projects can exhibit similar pride-driven characteristics.

- **Glory-Seeking:** Projects designed primarily to enhance the reputation of leaders or organizations rather than serve stakeholders
- **Control-Focused:** Projects that attempt to control outcomes through human effort alone without acknowledging dependence on God

- **Competition-Driven:** Projects motivated primarily by defeating competitors rather than serving customers
- **Legacy-Building:** Projects designed to create monuments to human achievement rather than lasting value for others
- **Resource-Hoarding:** Projects that concentrate resources and power rather than distributing benefits broadly

The Consequences of Misaligned Motivation

But the Lord came down to see the city and the tower which the sons of men had built. And the Lord said, "Indeed the people are *one and they all have one language, and this is what they begin to do; now nothing that they propose to do will be withheld from them."*

—Gen. 11:5-6

God's intervention wasn't motivated by jealousy or competition. It was motivated by mercy. He saw that human pride, unchecked by humility or dependence on God, would lead to even greater problems. The failure of the Tower of Babel prevented greater disasters that would have resulted from successful pride-driven projects.

Sometimes, project failures are actually God's protection from the negative consequences of success achieved through wrong motivations or methods.

The Path to Redemptive Failure

When projects fail due to pride or misaligned motivation, the path to redemption involves the following:

- **Humble Acknowledgment:** Recognizing how pride or wrong motives contributed to the failure
- **Repentant Reorientation:** Changing motivation from self-serving to others-serving
- **Relationship Restoration:** Rebuilding trust with stakeholders who were affected by the failure
- **Renewed Purpose:** Aligning future projects with God's purposes rather than human ambition
- **Resource Redistribution:** Using resources in ways that serve others rather than concentrating benefits

Finding God's Purpose in Project Setbacks

"For My thoughts are not your thoughts, nor are your ways My ways," says the Lord. "For as the heavens are higher than the earth, so are My ways higher than your ways, and My thoughts than your thoughts."

—Isa. 55:8-9

Not all project failures result from poor management or wrong motivations. Sometimes projects fail because God has different plans than we do. Sometimes setbacks are redirections rather than rejections. Sometimes delays are preparations for greater opportunities.

The key is learning to discern God's purposes in project setbacks and respond with faith rather than frustration.

Types of Redemptive Setbacks

- **Timing Adjustments:** Projects that are delayed until better opportunities or circumstances arise
- **Scope Refinements:** Projects that are scaled back to focus on more important objectives
- **Team Development:** Projects that experience challenges that build character and capability
- **Stakeholder Preparation:** Projects that are delayed until stakeholders are ready to receive and utilize the results
- **Resource Stewardship:** Projects that are modified to make better use of available resources
- **Relationship Building:** Projects that encounter obstacles that force better collaboration and communication

A Personal Example: The Failed Accounting Class

During my MBA program in project management, I encountered what I now fondly refer to as "the devil's arithmetic"—my accounting class. Despite having successfully managed complex technical projects for years, I found myself completely bewildered by balance sheets, cash flows, and the mysterious world of debits and credits. It was as if someone had decided that 2+2 should sometimes equal 5, depending on which side of the ledger you were sitting on.

I studied harder than I had for any project management certification. I attended every office hour. I joined study groups with fellow students who seemed to speak this foreign language of "GAAP principles" and "depreciation schedules." Yet when the final exam results came back, there it was in black and white—a failing grade that would require me to retake the entire course.

From an academic perspective, this was a complete failure. I had invested countless hours, significant tuition money, and considerable pride into a class I would now have to repeat. My graduation would be delayed, my GPA was damaged, and I was questioning whether someone who couldn't master basic accounting had any business pursuing an advanced degree in business management.

But God had different plans.

Being forced to retake the class meant I was assigned to a different professor—one whose teaching style clicked immediately with my project-oriented thinking. Instead of treating accounting as abstract number manipulation, she taught it as the financial project management of business operations.

Suddenly, cash flow statements became project timelines, and budget variance analysis became scope change management.

When Projects Fail: Redemption and Restoration   213

More importantly, the humbling experience of academic failure taught me lessons that no successful class ever could have. I learned to ask for help earlier, approach problems from different angles, and find mentors who could translate complex concepts into frameworks I could understand.

The most unexpected benefit came years later when I discovered the value of becoming "besties" with the finance and accounting teams at work. Because I had wrestled with their language and understood their perspective, I could build genuine relationships with the people who make project managers' lives either wonderful or miserable. These finance team relationships have become some of my most valuable professional assets.

Now, when I'm planning project budgets, the accounting team doesn't see me as just another project manager asking for money. They see me as someone who partners with them to understand and communicate with leadership project connections to depreciation schedules and cash flow risks. They proactively help me structure budgets that make sense from a financial controls perspective, saving me countless hours of revisions and reapprovals.

Even better, when I have to present to executives about NPV and IRR calculations, or CapEx vs. OpEx vs. RevEx implications, my finance friends give me the talking points that actually make sense to the C-suite. Instead of stumbling through technical explanations I half-understand, I can confidently explain why our project's internal rate of return justifies the capital investment and why the net present value calculations support our timeline recommendations. The CFO actually nods approvingly instead of looking like she's watching someone butcher her native language.

What initially appeared to be an embarrassing academic setback became preparation for much more effective financial leadership and some of the most valuable professional relationships in my career. The "failed" accounting class was actually essential training that equipped me to speak the CFO's language, understand the financial implications of every project decision, and build the finance team partnerships that make complex projects possible.

Lessons from Apparent Failure

- **God's Timing Is Perfect:** What seems like academic setbacks may be God's way of ensuring we get the right teacher and learning approach at the right time.

- **Investment Is Never Wasted:** Hours spent struggling with concepts, even unsuccessfully, create mental frameworks that make the second attempt much more effective.

- **Preparation Has Value:** Academic failures that don't achieve their original objectives (passing the first time) may still accomplish important preparatory work for deeper understanding.

- **Humility Brings Wisdom:** Academic failures can teach humility and dependence on God that make future learning and leadership more successful—especially when dealing with the devil's arithmetic.

- **Relationships Matter Most:** The relationships built during difficult experiences—including friendships with finance teams who can translate NPV and IRR into executive-friendly explanations—often matter more than the specific academic achievements.

The Failure Recovery Process

When projects fail, Christian project managers can follow a biblical process for recovery and restoration.

Step 1: Lament and Acknowledge Loss

To everything there is a season, a time for every purpose under heaven. A time to weep, and a time to laugh; a time to mourn, and a time to dance.

—Eccles. 3:1, 4

It's appropriate to acknowledge the genuine losses that result from project failure—wasted resources, disappointed stakeholders, missed opportunities, and personal disappointment. Biblical faith doesn't require pretending that failures don't hurt.

Step 2: Accept Responsibility Without Shame

> *If we confess our sins, He is faithful and just to forgive us our sins and to cleanse us from all unrighteousness.*
>
> —1 John 1:9

Take responsibility for your contributions to the failure without taking on shame for circumstances beyond your control. Acknowledge mistakes, learn from them, and accept God's forgiveness.

Step 3: Seek Wisdom and Learning

> *The heart of the prudent acquires knowledge, and the ear of the wise seeks knowledge.*
>
> —Prov. 18:15

Conduct thorough post-project reviews that identify lessons learned, process improvements, and capabilities developed. Focus on learning rather than blame assignment.

Step 4: Restore Relationships

> *Therefore if you bring your gift to the altar, and there remember that your brother has something against you, leave your gift there before the altar, and go your way.*

> *First be reconciled to your brother, and then come and offer your gift.*
>
> —Matt. 5:23-24

Address relationship damage that resulted from the project failure. Apologize where appropriate, make amends where possible, and rebuild trust through consistent behavior over time.

Step 5: Serve Others from Experience

> *Blessed* be *the God and Father of our Lord Jesus Christ, the Father of mercies and God of all comfort, who comforts us in all our tribulation, that we may be able to comfort those who are in any trouble, with the comfort with which we ourselves are comforted by God.*
>
> —2 Cor. 1:3-4

Use your experience with failure to help others navigate similar challenges. Mentor other project managers, share lessons learned, and provide encouragement to teams facing difficulties.

Step 6: Trust God for Redemption

> *And God* is *able to make all grace abound toward you, that you, always having all sufficiency in all* things, *may have an abundance for every good work.*
>
> —2 Cor. 9:8

Trust that God can bring good from even the most disappointing project failures. Remain open to how He might use your experience for His purposes and glory.

A Detailed Example: When Everything Went Wrong

Several years ago, I was managing what should have been a straightforward electronic health record upgrade for one of our healthcare organization's regions, which included multiple hospitals. The project had strong executive support, adequate budget, experienced team members, and proven technology. Everything pointed to success.

Then reality intervened.

The Cascade of Failures

- **Month 3:** Our primary vendor went through a major restructure, leading to support team changes and modified timelines.

- **Month 5:** The Performance Marketing Group representing the hospitals faced a Joint Commission survey that demanded immediate attention from clinical leadership, reducing their availability for project activities.

- **Month 7:** A ransomware attack on a nearby hospital prompted our security team to implement

When Projects Fail: Redemption and Restoration

additional requirements that affected our system architecture.

- **Month 9:** Our lead clinical analyst accepted a position with another organization, taking critical knowledge with her.

- **Month 11:** Budget cuts mandated by declining patient volumes forced a scope reduction that eliminated key functionality.

- **Month 13:** Go-live was postponed indefinitely when testing revealed integration problems that couldn't be resolved within the available timeline.

By any traditional measure, this project was a complete failure. We had missed every major milestone, exceeded the budget, lost key team members, and failed to deliver the promised functionality.

The Traditional Response

My initial reaction was classic project manager damage control.

- Develop revised timeline and budget estimates.
- Create detailed risk mitigation plans.
- Communicate extensively with frustrated stakeholders.
- Work longer hours to try to recover lost ground.
- Focus on protecting my professional reputation.

These activities were necessary but insufficient. They addressed symptoms without dealing with the deeper reality of failure.

The Biblical Response

After several sleepless nights and honest conversations with my mentor, I began applying biblical principles to failure recovery.

- *Lament:* I acknowledged the genuine disappointment and loss that the project failure represented for all stakeholders, including myself.

- *Responsibility:* I accepted responsibility for decisions that had contributed to the failure while not taking on guilt for circumstances beyond anyone's control.

- *Learning:* I conducted a thorough analysis of what had gone wrong and what could be learned from the experience.

- *Restoration:* I had honest conversations with stakeholders about the failure, apologized for my contributions, and worked to rebuild trust.

- *Service:* I used the experience to help other project managers who were facing similar challenges and improve our organizational project management processes.

- ***Trust:*** I chose to trust that God could bring good from this disappointing experience.

The Unexpected Redemption

Eighteen months later, the "failed" project became the foundation for a much more successful initiative.

- **Vendor Relationship:** The difficulties with our vendor led us to new vendor leadership, who provided better technology and superior support.

- **Team Development:** The challenges we faced together created stronger relationships and better collaboration skills among the remaining team members.

- **Organizational Learning:** The failure prompted improvements in project governance, risk management, and stakeholder engagement that benefited all subsequent projects.

- **Personal Growth:** The experience taught me humility, resilience, and dependence on God that made me a more effective leader.

- **Career Development:** My honest handling of the failure and focus on learning from it actually enhanced my reputation and led to greater opportunities.

What seemed like career-threatening failure became preparation for more significant leadership responsibilities.

Lessons from Redemptive Failure

- **Failure Reveals Character:** How we respond to failure reveals more about our character than how we handle success.

- **Transparency Builds Trust:** Honest acknowledgment of failure and responsibility builds credibility with stakeholders.

- **Learning Creates Value:** Knowledge gained from failure often proves more valuable than knowledge gained from success.

- **Humility Enables Growth:** Failure can teach humility and dependence on God that success rarely provides.

- **Relationships Endure:** The relationships built during difficult projects often outlast and outvalue the specific project outcomes.

Building Resilient Project Teams

The best approach to project failure is building teams that can recover quickly and learn effectively from setbacks.

Psychological Safety

Create environments where people feel safe acknowledging problems, asking for help, and admitting mistakes without fear of punishment or embarrassment.

Learning Orientation

Emphasize learning and growth over blame and punishment when problems occur. Treat failures as learning opportunities rather than performance deficiencies.

Shared Responsibility

Build team cultures where everyone takes ownership of project outcomes rather than pointing fingers when things go wrong.

Spiritual Foundation

Ground team identity in growth and opportunities to add testimonial value from the experience rather than project success, so failure doesn't devastate people's sense of worth or purpose.

Future Focus

Help teams see setbacks as preparation for future opportunities rather than final judgments on their capabilities.

Appropriate Boundaries with Grace

Model how to maintain project standards and team accountability while extending grace and support to struggling team members.

The Testimony of Transformed Failure

Some of the most powerful testimonies come from people who have experienced significant failures and found God's redemption in them. These stories provide hope and encouragement to others facing similar challenges.

When we handle project failures biblically—with humility, learning, and trust in God's sovereignty—we demonstrate that our identity and security come from God rather than from professional success. This provides a powerful witness to colleagues and stakeholders who may be watching how we respond to disappointment and setbacks.

Creating Failure Testimonies

When appropriate, share your failure experiences in ways that encourage others.

- **Be Honest:** Don't minimize the difficulty or disappointment of failure.
- **Take Responsibility:** Acknowledge your contributions without making excuses.
- **Highlight Learning:** Share specific lessons that benefited you and might help others.
- **Give God Glory:** Acknowledge how God brought good from difficult circumstances.
- **Offer Hope:** Help others see that failure doesn't disqualify them from future success.

- **Demonstrate Balance:** Show how you maintained appropriate standards while extending grace to yourself and others.

Practical Tools for Failure Recovery

The Failure Assessment Framework

When projects fail, use this framework to understand what happened.

- **Contributing Factors:** What circumstances, decisions, and events led to the failure?
- **Responsibility Analysis:** What was within your control versus beyond your control?
- **Learning Opportunities:** What insights can be gained that will improve future performance?
- **Relationship Impact:** How did the failure affect working relationships?
- **Redemption Potential:** How might God use this experience for good purposes?

The Restoration Action Plan

After a project failure, create a systematic plan for recovery.

Immediate Actions (Days 1-7):

- Acknowledge the failure honestly to key stakeholders.

- Take responsibility for your contributions.
- Begin damage control and communication.

Short-Term Actions (Weeks 1-4):
- Conduct thorough post-project analysis.
- Address relationship issues with affected parties.
- Develop lessons learned documentation.

Long-Term Actions (Months 1-6):
- Apply lessons learned to improve future projects.
- Mentor others facing similar challenges.
- Rebuild trust through consistent excellent performance.

The Learning Documentation Process

Capture insights from failure in ways that benefit future projects.

- **What Happened:** Factual timeline of events leading to failure
- **Why It Happened:** Root cause analysis of contributing factors
- **What We Learned:** Specific insights that will improve future performance
- **How We'll Apply It:** Concrete changes to processes, procedures, or practices

- **Who Should Know:** Distribution plan for sharing lessons with others

When Others Fail: Leading Through Team Member Setbacks

As project managers, we don't just handle our own failures; we help team members recover from theirs.

Creating Safe Failure Environments

- **Normalize Learning:** Treat failures as normal parts of growth and development.
- **Focus on Growth:** Emphasize what people learned rather than what went wrong.
- **Provide Support:** Offer resources and encouragement during difficult times.
- **Model Vulnerability:** Share your own failure experiences appropriately.
- **Celebrate Recovery:** Acknowledge when people bounce back from setbacks.

The Restoration Conversation

When team members fail, use this conversation framework.

- **Acknowledge:** "I know this didn't go as you hoped."

- **Affirm:** "This doesn't change my confidence in your abilities."
- **Analyze:** "What do you think we can learn from this experience?"
- **Act:** "How can I support you moving forward?"
- **Advance:** "What's our next step together?"

Maintaining Standards with Grace

Remember that biblical grace doesn't eliminate accountability.

- **Set Clear Expectations:** Communicate standards that honor God and serve stakeholders.
- **Follow Through Consistently:** Maintain accountability while showing respect for the person.
- **Provide Growth Opportunities:** Offer training, mentoring, and support for improvement.
- **Make Difficult Decisions:** When necessary, make personnel changes while maintaining dignity.
- **Protect the Team:** Ensure that one person's struggles don't harm the entire project.

The goal isn't to avoid all project failures. That's impossible in a fallen world with limited human capabilities. The goal is to respond to failures in ways that honor God, serve others, and build character that makes us more effective in future endeavors.

The Apostle Peter's denial didn't disqualify him from leadership; it prepared him for more effective leadership. Your project failures, handled biblically with both grace and appropriate boundaries, can do the same for you. In the next chapter, we'll explore how to deliver project results with excellence that honors God and creates lasting value for stakeholders.

But first, consider these reflection questions:

- How might your perspective on current project challenges change if you viewed them as potential preparation for future opportunities?

- What lessons from past failures could benefit other project managers in your organization?

- How could you create a safer environment for your team members to acknowledge and learn from mistakes while maintaining appropriate performance standards?

- What would change about your approach to project management if you truly believed that God can bring good from any failure?

- How can you better balance extending grace to struggling team members while maintaining project standards and protecting team morale?

Remember, failure is not the opposite of success; it's often the pathway to success. When we handle setbacks with faith, humility, appropriate boundaries, and learning, they become stepping stones to greater effectiveness and deeper character.

PART IV
Finishing Strong

The final phase of any project often determines whether temporary success becomes lasting impact. This part focuses on delivering excellence that honors God, celebrating achievements appropriately, and building a legacy that extends far beyond any single project. Discover how biblical principles of stewardship, gratitude, and mentorship can transform project closure into Kingdom building.

> **Oh My Stephen**
>
> *Most people do not listen with the intent to understand; they listen with the intent to reply.*
>
> —Stephen R. Covey,
> *The 7 Habits of Highly Effective People*

CHAPTER 10
Delivering Excellence for God's Glory

Real-World Application: Excellence in Government Healthcare IT

The following account is based on a true story from a recent healthcare IT implementation. Some details have been modified to protect confidentiality and illustrate key principles of applied best practices in a from-worst-case-to-best-case" scenario.

During a recent state-funded healthcare IT solution implementation, our team faced intense pressure from state government leadership to accelerate the go-live timeline to coincide with a legislative session where officials wanted to announce the new system as a key achievement in healthcare modernization. The proposed timeline would have required us to bypass comprehensive provider communication and engagement activities that were still in development, and would have eliminated time for meaningful stakeholder collaboration.

This presented a particularly challenging situation because the provider community was already experiencing significant trust issues with our agency. Just three months prior, the last major system module implementation had resulted in unforeseen post-go-live issues that severely impacted workflow efficiency for healthcare providers across the state. These providers had been extremely vocal about these impacts during public hearings and government engagement sessions, expressing frustration about being "informed rather than consulted" during the previous implementation.

The new healthcare IT solution represented an even more significant change for providers, requiring modifications to existing workflows, new system interfaces, and integration with multiple external platforms. The stakes were high. Successful implementation would improve healthcare delivery efficiency across the state, while failure could further erode provider trust and potentially impact patient care.

As an industry leader in this space, our team felt strongly that provider engagement was too critical to rush, especially given our recent implementation challenges. The provider community's trust in our ability to deliver stable, well-tested solutions was already fragile. But we also understood the political pressures driving the accelerated timeline request and the genuine desire of state leadership to demonstrate progress on healthcare modernization initiatives.

The Excellence Decision

Rather than simply refusing the timeline request or capitulating to political pressure, we took a third approach that demonstrated excellence in both technical delivery and stakeholder service.

- **We presented options with clear trade-offs:** Instead of just saying no to the accelerated timeline, we presented three options with detailed analysis of risks, costs, and benefits for each approach. We included specific metrics on provider satisfaction, potential workflow disruption, and system stability based on lessons learned from our previous implementation.

- **We recommended the excellent approach:** We clearly advocated for a phased implementation timeline that would ensure comprehensive provider engagement and thorough testing, explaining our reasoning in terms of patient safety, provider trust, and long term program success. We emphasized how the previous implementation's challenges demonstrated the critical importance of stakeholder collaboration and risk mitigation through gradual deployment. However, we also prepared alternative risk mitigation strategies should the state leadership decide to proceed with a "big bang" approach, ensuring we could support whatever decision was made while still protecting provider and patient interests.

- **We offered creative alternatives:** We proposed ways to provide the Legislature with meaningful progress updates without compromising implementation quality, including demonstrations of system capabilities in controlled environments, sharing of pilot testing results, and testimonials from early adopter providers who were participating in our collaborative development process.

- **We maintained flexibility:** We committed to accelerating the timeline if we could do so without compromising quality or stakeholder engagement, and we provided biweekly updates on our progress toward that goal.

The Results

The state leadership team chose to extend the timeline after understanding the risks of acceleration and the potential for repeating previous implementation challenges. Instead of a rushed inform-only approach, we implemented a comprehensive provider engagement strategy that included the following:

- **Stakeholder Advisory Groups:** Formation of provider committees representing different specialties and practice sizes to guide implementation decisions

- **Pilot Testing Program:** A voluntary pilot program with willing providers who helped identify workflow issues before full deployment

- **Comprehensive Communication Plan:** Multi-channel communication strategy, including webinars, site visits, and peer-to-peer learning sessions

- **Gradual Rollout Approach:** Phased implementation allowing for real-world feedback and system refinements

The system went live successfully with minimal disruption to patient care and significantly higher provider satisfaction scores than our previous implementation. The pilot testing phase identified and resolved 12 critical workflow issues that would have caused significant problems in a rushed deployment.

Six months later, the State Health Director sent a letter to the entire project team that said this:

Your commitment to stakeholder engagement over political expediency has restored provider confidence in our modernization efforts. The collaborative approach you insisted upon has created a system that providers actually want to use, and patients are already benefiting from improved care coordination. Thank you for prioritizing long-term success over short-term political wins.

Lessons About Excellence

> *Be strong and of good courage; do not be afraid, nor be dismayed, for the Lord your God is with you wherever you go.*
>
> —Josh. 1:9

Excellence Requires Courage

It takes courage to advocate for stakeholder engagement when political leaders are pressuring for speed or visible deliverables. But when we stand firm on principles that serve others well, God provides the strength and wisdom needed to navigate difficult conversations and defend quality standards.

- **Excellence Learns from Failure:** "And we know that all things work together for good to those who love God, to those who are the called according to *His* purpose" (Rom. 8:28).

  Our previous implementation challenges provided crucial insights that informed our decision to prioritize provider engagement. Just as Scripture corrects and instructs us, failures become opportunities for learning and growth when we approach them with humility and a commitment to improvement.

- **Excellence Serves All Stakeholders:** "And whatever you do, do it heartily, as to the Lord and not to men, knowing that from the Lord you will receive the reward of the inheritance; for you serve the Lord Christ" (Col. 3:23-24).

  We found ways to serve both the political leadership's need for progress demonstration and the provider community's need for meaningful collaboration. When we work as unto the Lord, He provides wisdom to navigate competing demands while maintaining integrity and serving all stakeholders well.

- **Excellence Rebuilds Trust:** "With all lowliness and gentleness, with longsuffering, bearing with one another in love, endeavoring to keep the unity of the spirit in the bond of peace" (Eph. 4:2-3).

  Taking the time to properly engage stakeholders helped restore confidence that previous rushed implementations had damaged. By approaching providers with humility, patience, and genuine care for their concerns, we were able to rebuild relationships and create unity around our shared goal of improving healthcare delivery.

- **Excellence Honors God:** "Let your light so shine before men, that they may see your good works and glorify your Father in heaven" (Matt. 5:16).

When our work reflects God's character through honest communication, genuine service to others, and stewardship of public resources, it becomes a form of worship and witness in the government sector. Excellence in our professional conduct points others to the source of our motivation and standards.

CHAPTER 11
Celebrating Success and Giving Glory

Then David and all the house of Israel played music *before the Lord on all kinds of* instruments *of fir wood, on harps, on stringed instruments, on tambourines, on sistrums, and on cymbals.*

—2 Sam. 6:5

Jesus's Triumphal Entry: Recognizing Achievements Appropriately

Then they brought the colt to Jesus and threw their clothes on it, and He sat on it. And many spread their clothes on the road, and others cut down leafy branches from the trees and spread them *on the road. Then those who went before and those who followed cried out, saying: "Hosanna! Blessed* is *He who comes in the name of the Lord!"*

—Mark 11:7-9

Jesus's triumphal entry into Jerusalem provides a fascinating study in how to handle recognition and celebration appropriately. The crowds were celebrating His miraculous works and acknowledging Him as the Messiah. By any measure, this was a moment of tremendous public acclaim and project success.

Yet Jesus's response was notably different from how most leaders handle success.

- **He Remained Humble:** Jesus didn't let the celebration go to His head or change His mission focus.

- **He Stayed Mission-Focused:** Even during the celebration, He was preparing for the greater work of redemption.

- **He Gave Glory to God:** His actions consistently pointed people toward God rather than toward Himself.

- **He Served Others:** The celebration didn't become about serving His ego but about serving God's purposes.

This model provides guidance for Christian project managers about how to celebrate project successes in ways that honor God, recognize contributors, and build momentum for future achievements.

The Biblical Purpose of Celebration

Celebration in Scripture serves multiple purposes beyond just recognizing achievement.

- **Remembering God's Faithfulness:** Celebrations help people remember how God has provided and blessed their efforts.

- **Building Community:** Shared celebrations strengthen relationships and create unity among team members.

- **Creating Momentum:** Acknowledging success builds confidence and motivation for future challenges.

- **Teaching Lessons:** Celebrations provide opportunities to share what was learned and how others can benefit.

- **Giving Testimony:** Success stories become testimonies that encourage others and bring glory to God.

Case Study: Joshua's Stones of Remembrance—Documenting Lessons Learned

And Joshua said to them: "Cross over before the ark of the Lord your God into the midst of the Jordan, and each one of you take up a stone on his shoulder, according to the number of the tribes of the children of Israel, that this may be a sign among you when your children ask in time to come, saying, 'What do these stones mean *to you?'"*

—Josh. 4:5-6

When the Israelites successfully crossed the Jordan River into the Promised Land, God instructed Joshua to create a permanent memorial of the achievement. Twelve stones were taken from the riverbed and set up as a monument that would remind future generations of God's faithfulness and power.

This wasn't just about celebrating a single achievement. It was about creating a learning resource that would benefit people for generations to come. The stones served as the following:

- **Historical Record:** Documentation of what God had accomplished through His people

- **Teaching Tool:** A visual aid that would help parents explain God's faithfulness to their children

- **Faith Builder:** A reminder that God can overcome seemingly impossible obstacles

- **Legacy Creator:** A monument that would inspire future generations to trust God for their own challenges

Modern project managers can apply these principles by creating celebrations and documentation that serve similar purposes for their organizations.

The Documentation Discipline

Then those men, when they had seen the sign that Jesus did, said, "This is truly the Prophet who is to come into the world."

—John 6:14

Every successful project should include comprehensive documentation that captures not just what was accomplished but how it was accomplished and what lessons were learned. This documentation serves multiple purposes.

- **Organizational Learning:** Future projects can benefit from methods and solutions that worked well.

- **Team Recognition:** Documentation preserves the record of individual and team contributions.

- **Process Improvement:** Lessons learned help refine organizational project management capabilities.

- **Stakeholder Communication:** Success stories can be shared with leadership and other stakeholders.

- **Personal Development:** Documentation helps team members track their own growth and achievements.

The STONE Documentation Framework

- *Successes:* What went well and why it worked
- *Team Contributions:* Who did what and how they contributed to success
- *Obstacles Overcome:* What challenges were faced and how were they resolved
- *New Capabilities:* What skills, processes, or systems were developed
- *Eternal Lessons:* What insights can benefit future projects and other teams

This framework ensures that project closure includes both the celebration of achievements and the capture of learning that will benefit future work.

The Gratitude Gap: Why Christian PMs Must Celebrate Differently

Oh, give thanks to the Lord, for He is *good! For His mercy* endures *forever.*

—Ps. 107:1

There's a significant gap between how secular organizations celebrate success and how Christian project managers should approach celebration. Secular celebrations often focus on human achievement, competitive advantage, and personal advancement. Biblical celebrations focus on God's faithfulness, team contributions, and service to others.

> **Oh My Stephen**
>
> *We judge ourselves by our intentions and others by their behavior.*
>
> —Stephen R. Covey,
> *The 7 Habits of Highly Effective People*

The Secular Celebration Model

Traditional project celebrations often exhibit the following characteristics:

- **Leader-Focused:** The project manager or senior leadership receives most of the recognition.
- **Achievement-Oriented:** The focus is on what was accomplished rather than how it serves others.
- **Competition-Driven:** Success is measured by beating competitors or exceeding previous performance.

- **Individual-Centered:** Recognition goes primarily to star performers rather than team contributors.
- **Temporary:** Celebrations are brief events rather than ongoing practices of gratitude.

The Biblical Celebration Model

Christian project managers should approach celebration differently.

- **God-Honoring:** Recognition begins with acknowledging God's provision and blessing.
- **Team-Focused:** Recognition flows to team members who did the actual work.
- **Service-Oriented:** The focus is on how success serves stakeholders and advances God's Kingdom.
- **Relationship-Building:** Celebrations strengthen relationships and build community.
- **Legacy-Creating:** Celebrations create lasting records and ongoing practices of gratitude.

A Personal Example: Celebrating the Right Way

A few years ago, our team completed a major implementation of a patient engagement platform that significantly improved patient satisfaction scores and reduced administrative burden for clinical staff. The project finished ahead of schedule and under budget, with stakeholder satisfaction ratings above 95 percent.

Revenue Cycle leadership wanted to hold a celebration dinner where I would receive an award for outstanding project management. While I appreciated the recognition, I felt this approach missed the opportunity to celebrate appropriately. Instead, I proposed a different celebration format.

- **Team Recognition Event:** Rather than focusing on individual achievement, we held an event that recognized specific contributions from every team member.

- **Stakeholder Testimony:** Patients and clinical staff shared stories about how the new system had improved their experiences.

- **Lessons Learned Sharing:** We documented and shared key insights that would help future projects succeed.

- **Service Dedication:** We dedicated the success to serving our patients and community better, acknowledging that excellent healthcare technology is ultimately about serving others.

God's Glory with Biblical Discernment

When it was my turn to share my experience, I had to exercise biblical discernment about how to acknowledge God's provision. In that moment, through Holy Spirit discernment, I was able to "read the room" and sense that I could boldly praise God with my team. I began by acknowledging God's provision and guidance throughout the project, and my testimony seemed to empower other believers who were on the team to also share their praise to God as well. However, this is not always the case. "To everything *there is* a season, a time for every purpose under heaven. . . . A time to keep silence, and a time to speak" (Eccles. 3:1, 7).

Sometimes the Holy Spirit—that still small voice—tells me in wisdom when it is not the time to speak boldly about my faith or of God in front of others. True believers read and know the Word of God and therefore know the voice of our Good Shepherd. "My sheep hear My voice, and I know them, and they follow Me" (John 10:27). As we learn to be like Christ, who knew when to speak and when to remain silent, we must obey what the Holy Spirit tells us to do, or not do, depending on the situation. "But the Helper, the Holy Spirit, whom the Father will send in My name, He will teach you all things, and bring to your remembrance all things that I said to you" (John 14:26). This divine wisdom helps us navigate workplace celebrations in ways that honor God while being sensitive to our colleagues and the appropriate timing for bold witness versus quiet faithfulness.

The Results of Appropriate Celebration

This approach to celebration had several positive outcomes.

- **Team Morale:** Team members felt genuinely appreciated and valued for their specific contributions.

- **Organizational Learning:** Sharing the lessons learned helped other departments improve their own project approaches.

- **Stakeholder Engagement:** Patients and staff felt more connected to the organization and more supportive of future improvements.

- **Cultural Impact:** The celebration model became a template for how other departments recognize achievements.

- **Personal Growth:** I experienced the joy of seeing others receive recognition while knowing that the success honored God.

Practical Celebration Strategies

The Three-Tiered Recognition Model

1. **Individual Recognition:** Acknowledge specific contributions that team members made to project success.

2. **Team Recognition:** Celebrate collective achievements that required collaboration and mutual support.

3. **Organizational Recognition:** Share success stories that demonstrate organizational values and capabilities.

The PRAISE Celebration Framework

- *Purpose Connection:* Connect project success to the larger organizational mission and values.

- *Recognition Distribution:* Ensure recognition flows to everyone who contributed to success.

- *Achievement Documentation:* Create permanent records of what was accomplished and how.

- *Impact Communication:* Share stories about how success benefits stakeholders and the community.

- *Stewardship Acknowledgment:* Recognize responsible use of resources and opportunities.

- *Eternal Perspective:* Acknowledge God's provision and guidance throughout the project.

Creative Celebration Ideas

- **Success Stories Video:** Create a video compilation of stakeholder testimonials about project impact.

- **Team Contribution Wall:** Display specific recognition for each team member's contributions.

- **Lessons Learned Workshop:** Turn project closure into a learning event that benefits the entire organization.

- **Service Project:** Celebrate success by undertaking a community service project as a team.

- **Mentoring Initiative:** Use project success as a platform for mentoring other project managers and teams.

- **Gratitude Journal:** Create a shared journal where team members can express gratitude for each other's contributions.

Advanced Celebration Approaches

The Story-Based Celebration

Rather than just listing achievements, create compelling narratives such as the one below to help people understand the human impact of project success.

When Mrs. Rodriguez first tried to schedule her follow-up appointment using our old system, she had to call during business hours, wait on hold for 20 minutes, and then coordinate with three different departments. Last week, she used our new patient portal to schedule her appointment on her smartphone in less than two minutes while waiting for her granddaughter's soccer practice to end. That's the kind of difference our project team has made for thousands of patients like Mrs. Rodriguez.

The Stakeholder Journey Celebration

Map out how different stakeholder groups experienced the project and then celebrate the positive transformation.

- **Before the Project:** What challenges and frustrations did stakeholders face?
- **During the Project:** How did stakeholders experience the change process?
- **After the Project:** What improvements are stakeholders now experiencing?
- **Future Impact:** How will stakeholders continue to benefit from project success?

The Values-Based Celebration

Connect project achievements to organizational or team values that were demonstrated.

- **Integrity:** How did the team maintain honesty and transparency throughout the project?
- **Excellence:** What examples of going above and beyond did team members demonstrate?
- **Service:** How did project decisions prioritize stakeholder needs over convenience?

- **Collaboration:** What examples of teamwork and mutual support emerged during the project?
- **Innovation:** How did the team find creative solutions to challenging problems?

When Success Creates Temptation

Pride goes before destruction, and a haughty spirit before a fall.

—Prov. 16:18

Project success can create spiritual temptations that Christian project managers must navigate carefully.

- **Pride:** Taking credit for results that required God's blessing and team effort.
- **Complacency:** Assuming that past success guarantees future success without continued diligence.
- **Comparison:** Using success to feel superior to other project managers or teams.
- **Ambition:** Leveraging success for personal advancement rather than greater service.
- **Control:** Believing that success proves we can control outcomes through our own effort.

Staying Humble in Success

- **Remember Dependence:** Acknowledge that ultimate success depends on God's blessing, not just human effort.
- **Share Credit:** Ensure that recognition flows to team members and other contributors.
- **Learn Continuously:** Treat success as a learning opportunity rather than a final achievement.
- **Serve Others:** Use success as a platform for helping others achieve their own success.
- **Maintain Perspective:** Remember that earthly success is temporary while eternal values are lasting.

The Multiplication Effect of Appropriate Celebration

When Christian project managers celebrate success appropriately, it creates positive effects that extend far beyond the immediate project.

- **Team Development:** Team members who feel genuinely appreciated are more likely to contribute excellent effort to future projects.
- **Organizational Culture:** Appropriate celebration models help create organizational cultures that value both excellence and humility.

- **Stakeholder Relationships:** Celebrations that focus on service to others strengthen relationships with stakeholders.

- **Personal Growth:** Giving credit to others while acknowledging God's provision develops character and leadership capability.

- **Witness Opportunity:** Celebrating in ways that honor God creates opportunities to share faith with colleagues.

Building a Legacy of Celebration

Every celebration should contribute to a legacy of gratitude, learning, and service that extends beyond the current project.

- **Create Traditions:** Establish celebration practices that become part of organizational culture.

- **Document Stories:** Preserve success stories that can inspire and instruct future teams.

- **Develop Others:** Use celebrations as opportunities to recognize and develop emerging leaders.

- **Build Relationships:** Strengthen connections that will support future collaboration.

- **Honor God:** Consistently acknowledge God's role in success and blessing.

The Failure-to-Success Celebration

Some of the most meaningful celebrations involve projects that overcame significant obstacles or recovered from apparent failures.

Celebrating Resilience

When projects succeed after facing major challenges, celebrations should acknowledge the following:

- **The Journey:** Obstacles that were overcome and how the team persevered
- **The Growth:** How team members developed through facing difficulties
- **The Learning:** What insights were gained that will benefit future projects
- **The Character:** How team members demonstrated integrity, courage, and commitment
- **The Providence:** How God's guidance and provision were evident throughout

A Personal Example: The Comeback Project

Three years ago, our team inherited a troubled IT healthcare project that had been stalled for six months due to vendor conflicts and stakeholder resistance. When we took over, morale was low, budgets were exhausted, and stakeholders had lost confidence in the technology solution.

Rather than celebrating when we finally achieved go-live success, we designed a celebration that acknowledged the journey.

- **"From Struggle to Success" Timeline:** We created a visual timeline showing how the project had progressed from challenges to achievements.

- **"Heroes of Recovery" Recognition:** We specifically recognized team members who had gone above and beyond to turn the project around.

- **"Lessons from the Valley" Documentation:** We captured insights gained during the difficult period that would help future projects avoid similar problems.

- **"New Beginnings" Vision:** We used the celebration to launch a discussion about how lessons learned would improve future project approaches.

The celebration became more meaningful because it acknowledged both the difficulties we overcame and the character we developed through the struggle.

Cultural Considerations in Celebration

Different organizational cultures and individual personalities require different celebration approaches.

High-Context vs. Low-Context Cultures

- **High-Context:** Emphasize relationship-building, storytelling, and communal recognition.
- **Low-Context:** Focus on specific achievements, clear metrics, and individual contributions.

Extroverted vs. Introverted Preferences

- **Extroverted:** Public recognition, group celebrations, verbal appreciation
- **Introverted:** Private recognition, written appreciation, meaningful one-on-one conversations

Hierarchical vs. Egalitarian Organizations

- **Hierarchical:** Ensure recognition flows through appropriate authority structures.
- **Egalitarian:** Emphasize peer recognition and collaborative achievements.

Individual vs. Collective Orientations

- **Individual:** Recognize specific personal contributions and achievements.
- **Collective:** Emphasize team success and shared accomplishments.

Practical Tools for Celebration Planning

The Celebration Planning Worksheet

- **Project Overview:** What was accomplished and why it matters
- **Key Contributors:** Who should be recognized and for what specific contributions
- **Success Metrics:** What measurable outcomes demonstrate project success
- **Stakeholder Impact:** How project success benefited different stakeholder groups
- **Lessons Learned:** What insights should be captured and shared
- **God's Role:** How God's provision and guidance were evident throughout the project
- **Future Application:** How successful lessons will benefit future projects

The Recognition Mapping Process

Create a comprehensive map of everyone who contributed to project success.

- **Core Team Members:** People who worked on the project directly
- **Supporting Cast:** People who provided resources, expertise, or assistance

- **Stakeholder Champions:** People who advocated for the project and facilitated success
- **Behind-the-Scenes Contributors:** People whose work enabled project success indirectly
- **Leadership Support:** People who provided authority, resources, and organizational backing

The Gratitude Expression Framework

- **Specific:** Describe exactly what the person did and why it mattered.
- **Sincere:** Express genuine appreciation rather than generic praise.
- **Timely:** Provide recognition while achievements are still fresh.
- **Public:** Share appreciation in front of peers when appropriate.
- **Personal:** Connect recognition to the individual's values and motivations.

Building an Organizational Celebration Culture

Individual celebration practices are important, but the greatest impact comes from building organizational cultures where appropriate celebration is the norm.

Leadership Modeling

- **Demonstrate Humility:** Show how to accept recognition gracefully while giving credit to others.
- **Share Glory:** Consistently point recognition toward team members and God's provision.
- **Tell Stories:** Regularly share stories about project successes that inspire others.
- **Create Traditions:** Establish celebration practices that become part of the organizational DNA.

Systems and Processes

- **Documentation Standards:** Require thorough documentation of successes and lessons learned.
- **Recognition Programs:** Create formal mechanisms for acknowledging excellent project results.
- **Story Sharing:** Provide regular opportunities for teams to share success stories.
- **Learning Integration:** Connect celebration activities to organizational learning and improvement.

Cultural Values

- **Excellence *and* Humility:** Celebrate high performance while maintaining appropriate humility.

- **Individual *and* Team:** Recognize both personal contributions and collective achievements.
- **Achievement *and* Character:** Acknowledge both results delivered and values demonstrated.
- **Present *and* Future:** Celebrate current success while building momentum for future projects.

The Spiritual Discipline of Celebration

Rejoice always, pray without ceasing, in everything give thanks; for this is the will of God in Christ Jesus for you.

—1 Thess. 5:16-18

For Christian project managers, celebration is more than a management practice. It's a spiritual discipline that does the following:

- **Cultivates Gratitude:** Regular celebration develops a heart of thanksgiving toward God and others.
- **Builds Faith:** Remembering God's faithfulness in past projects builds confidence for future challenges.
- **Strengthens Community:** Shared celebration creates bonds that transcend professional relationships.

- **Gives Testimony:** Celebrating God's provision creates opportunities to share faith with colleagues.
- **Develops Character:** Learning to celebrate others' achievements builds humility and generosity.

Celebration is not optional. It's an essential component of project management that builds momentum, strengthens relationships, and creates organizational learning. When done biblically, celebration becomes a form of worship that honors God while serving others.

In the final chapter, we'll explore how to build a legacy of leadership that extends far beyond any single project, thus creating a lasting impact through mentoring, character development, and Kingdom building.

But first, consider these reflection questions:

- How might your project celebrations change if you focused first on honoring God and serving others?
- What stories from your current or recent projects could inspire and instruct others?
- How could you use celebration as an opportunity to develop and recognize emerging leaders?
- What traditions could you establish that would create a lasting legacy of gratitude and learning?

Remember, every project success is ultimately a gift from God that should be received with gratitude, shared with others, and leveraged for greater service. Celebration isn't about taking credit; it's about giving glory where glory is due while building momentum for future Kingdom work.

CHAPTER 12
Legacy Leadership

I have fought the good fight, I have finished the race, I have kept the faith. Finally, there is laid up for me the crown of righteousness, which the Lord, the righteous Judge, will give to me on that Day, and not to me only but also to all who have loved His appearing.

—2 Tim. 4:7-8

Mentoring the Next Generation of Faith-Based Leaders

Near the end of his life, the Apostle Paul wasn't focused on his own achievements or legacy. Instead, he was investing in Timothy, Titus, and other young leaders who would carry on the work after he was gone. His letters reveal a leader who understood that true success isn't measured by what you accomplish personally but by what you enable others to accomplish after you're no longer there.

And the things that you have heard from me among many witnesses, commit these to faithful men who will be able to teach others also.

—2 Tim. 2:2

This verse describes a multiplication strategy that goes far beyond traditional mentoring. Paul invested in Timothy, who would invest in "faithful men," who would invest in "others also." That's four generations of leadership development from one mentoring relationship.

Christian project managers have the same opportunity. Every project we manage is a chance to develop people who will go on to lead excellent projects of their own. Every team member we invest in becomes a potential mentor for future team members. Every principle we teach gets multiplied through the people we develop.

The Multiplication Principle of Leadership Development

Traditional leadership development focuses on building individual capabilities. Biblical leadership development focuses on building people who build other people. The goal isn't just to create competent project managers. It's to create competent project managers who are passionate about developing other competent project managers.

This multiplication effect is what transforms individual project success into organizational transformation and Kingdom impact.

What to Transfer to Future Leaders

- **Technical Skills:** The project management methodologies, tools, and techniques that enable excellent project delivery

- **Leadership Principles:** The character-based leadership principles that create trust, motivate teams, and build relationships

- **Spiritual Practices:** The prayer, worship, and biblical study practices that keep project managers connected to God's purposes

- **Wisdom Insights:** The hard-earned lessons about navigating organizational politics, handling difficult stakeholders, and making tough decisions

- **Kingdom Perspective:** The understanding that project management is ministry and that excellence in work is an act of worship

Your Project Portfolio in Eternity's Perspective

For we must all appear before the judgment seat of Christ, that each one may receive the things done *in the body, according to what he has done, whether good or bad.*

—2 Cor. 5:10

Imagine standing before Christ and reviewing your project portfolio from eternity's perspective. What questions do you think He might ask?

Will He ask about your budget performance? Probably not specifically, though faithful stewardship of resources would certainly matter.

Will He ask about your schedule adherence? Again, probably not specifically, though reliability and keeping commitments would be important.

Will He ask about your technical achievements? It's unlikely unless those achievements served His Kingdom purposes.

More likely, He'll ask questions like these:

- How did you serve others through your project management work?
- What kind of leader did you become through the challenges you faced?
- How did you develop the people I entrusted to your leadership?
- Did your work reflect My character and advance My Kingdom?
- How did you use the gifts and opportunities I gave you?

This eternal perspective should shape how we approach every project decision, every team interaction, and every opportunity for leadership development.

The Portfolio Review Process

Christian project managers should regularly review their project portfolio from an eternal perspective.

- **Service Assessment:** How did this project serve others? What needs were met? What problems were solved? How were people's lives improved?

- **Character Development:** What character qualities did this project develop in you and your team members? How did challenges build faith, patience, courage, or other virtues?

- **Relationship Impact:** What relationships were strengthened through this project? How did working together build trust, understanding, and mutual respect?

- **Kingdom Advancement:** How did this project advance God's Kingdom? What Kingdom values were demonstrated? How did the work point others toward God?

- **Leadership Legacy:** Who was developed through this project? What capabilities were built? How are those people now serving others in their own leadership roles?

A Personal Example: The Legacy Perspective

Several years ago, I managed an implementation of a new clinical documentation system that was technically successful but relationally challenging. The project finished on time and within budget, but team morale was low, and several team members requested transfers to other projects afterward.

From a traditional project management perspective, this was a success. All objectives were met, stakeholders were satisfied, and the system performed as designed. But from an eternal perspective, I failed in significant ways. I focused so intently on project deliverables that I neglected team development. I was so concerned about meeting deadlines that I created a stressful environment that didn't reflect God's character. I achieved project success but failed at leadership development.

That experience taught me this important lesson: Successful projects that don't develop people and strengthen relationships are ultimately unsuccessful from God's perspective. Since then, I've made team development and relationship-building as important as technical delivery in every project I manage.

The Long-Term View

- *Projects are temporary; relationships are permanent.* The systems we build will eventually be replaced, but the relationships we build can last for eternity.

- *Deliverables serve temporary needs; character serves eternal purposes.* The solutions we create solve immediate problems, but the character we develop serves God's eternal purposes.

- *Technical skills become obsolete; leadership principles remain relevant.* The specific technologies we master will become outdated, but the leadership principles we learn and teach remain valuable across generations.

- *Individual achievements are limited; multiplication effects are unlimited.* What we accomplish personally is limited by our own capabilities, but what we accomplish through developing others has unlimited potential.

The Mentoring Process

Effective mentoring in project management requires intentional structure and ongoing commitment.

Phase 1: Assessment and Selection

- **Identify Potential:** Look for team members who demonstrate character, competence, and coachability—the three C's of leadership potential.

- **Assess Readiness:** Determine whether potential mentees are ready for the time commitment and growth challenges that effective mentoring requires.

- **Mutual Commitment:** Establish clear expectations and mutual commitment to the mentoring relationship.

Phase 2: Foundation Building

- **Character Development:** Focus first on character qualities that underlie effective leadership—integrity, humility, service orientation, and dependence on God.

- **Relationship-Building:** Invest time in knowing mentees personally, understanding their goals, fears, and motivations.

- **Vision Casting:** Help mentees understand how their project management calling can serve God's Kingdom purposes.

Phase 3: Skill Development

- **Progressive Responsibility:** Give mentees increasing responsibility with corresponding support and guidance.

- **Real-World Application:** Provide opportunities to apply new skills in actual project situations with coaching and feedback.

- **Failure Processing:** Help mentees learn from mistakes without being devastated by them.

Phase 4: Independence and Multiplication

- **Gradual Release:** Transition from directing to coaching to consulting as mentees develop competence and confidence.
- **Multiplication Expectation:** Encourage mentees to begin mentoring others as they develop their own capabilities.
- **Ongoing Relationship:** Maintain long-term relationships that provide ongoing support and accountability.

Creating Your Leadership Development Plan

Every Christian project manager should have a personal plan for developing other leaders.

Your Development Goals

- How many people will you intentionally mentor over the next five years?
- What specific capabilities will you focus on developing in others?
- How will you measure success in leadership development?

- What resources will you invest in developing others?

Your Development Methods

- **Formal Mentoring:** Structured relationships with specific goals and regular meetings
- **Project-Based Development:** Using actual projects as leadership development opportunities
- **Group Development:** Leading workshops, training sessions, or study groups
- **Resource Sharing:** Providing books, articles, and other learning resources
- **Network Building:** Connecting developing leaders with other mentors and opportunities

Your Development Legacy

- *What kind of leaders do you want to develop?* Character-based, service-oriented, biblically grounded, technically competent, relationally skilled
- *How will your mentees be different because of your investment in them?* More effective, more godly, more committed to developing others
- *What will your mentees accomplish that they wouldn't have accomplished without your mentoring?* Better projects, stronger teams, greater Kingdom impact

The Character Foundation of Legacy Leadership

But you, O man of God, flee these things and pursue righteousness, godliness, faith, love, patience, gentleness.
—1 Tim. 6:11

Legacy leadership isn't built on technical competence or professional achievements. It's built on character that reflects God's nature and serves others sacrificially.

The Character Qualities of Legacy Leaders

- **Integrity:** Consistency between private character and public behavior

- **Humility:** Recognition that all abilities and opportunities come from God

- **Service:** Commitment to serving others rather than being served

- **Faith:** Dependence on God's wisdom and provision rather than human capability alone

- **Love:** Genuine care for people that goes beyond professional relationships

- **Patience:** Willingness to invest time in developing others even when progress is slow

- **Gentleness:** Strength under control that corrects without crushing

Character Development Practices

- **Daily Scripture Study:** Regular engagement with God's Word that shapes thinking and decision-making
- **Prayer and Worship:** Ongoing communication with God that maintains proper perspective and dependence
- **Accountability Relationships:** Trusted relationships that provide feedback and correction when needed
- **Service Opportunities:** Regular involvement in serving others outside of professional responsibilities
- **Continuous Learning:** Ongoing commitment to growing in wisdom, knowledge, and spiritual maturity
- **Reflection and Evaluation:** Regular assessment of character growth and areas needing development

Building Organizations That Develop Leaders

Individual mentoring is important, but the greatest impact comes from building organizational cultures that systematically develop leaders.

Organizational Systems for Leadership Development

- **Formal Mentoring Programs:** Structured programs that pair experienced leaders with developing leaders
- **Leadership Rotations:** Opportunities for potential leaders to experience different aspects of project management and organizational leadership
- **Cross-Functional Projects:** Projects that expose developing leaders to different parts of the organization and different types of challenges
- **Leadership Training:** Formal training programs that build both technical and leadership capabilities
- **Performance Feedback:** Regular feedback systems that help people understand their strengths and development needs

Cultural Elements That Support Leadership Development

- **Growth Mindset:** Organizational belief that people can develop and improve rather than being limited by current capabilities.
- **Learning from Failure:** A Culture that treats mistakes as learning opportunities rather than reasons for punishment.

- **Service Orientation:** Organizational commitment to serving others rather than just achieving financial or competitive objectives.
- **Character Emphasis:** Recognition and reward systems that value character development alongside performance achievement.
- **Kingdom Perspective:** Understanding that work serves God's purposes and contributes to His Kingdom.

The Ultimate Project: Building God's Kingdom

And Jesus came and spoke to them, saying, "All authority has been given to Me in heaven and on earth. Go therefore and make disciples of all the nations, baptizing them in the name of the Father and of the Son and of the Holy Spirit, teaching them to observe all things that I have commanded you; and lo, I am with you always, even to the end of the age."
—Matt. 28:18-20

The Great Commission is the ultimate project for every Christian, including Christian project managers. We're called to make disciples—to develop people who follow Jesus and help others follow Jesus too. This calling transforms how we think about our professional work. We're not just managing projects; we're participating in God's project of building His Kingdom. Every person we develop, every relationship we build, and every act of service we perform contributes to this ultimate objective.

Kingdom-Building Through Project Management

- **Character Modeling:** Demonstrating Christ-like character in professional relationships becomes a testimony to God's transforming power.

- **Excellence as Worship:** Delivering excellent work that serves others well becomes an act of worship that brings glory to God.

- **People Development:** Developing others' capabilities and character contributes to their spiritual growth and Kingdom impact.

- **Service Orientation:** Using projects to serve others rather than just achieve organizational objectives advances Kingdom values.

- **Stewardship Practice:** Managing resources faithfully demonstrates trustworthiness with greater responsibilities.

The Eternal Significance of Temporal Work

And whatever you do in word or deed, do all in the name of the Lord Jesus, giving thanks to God the Father through Him.

—Col. 3:17

When we approach project management as ministry, our temporal work gains eternal significance.

- Every project becomes an opportunity to serve others in Jesus's name.
- Every team interaction becomes a chance to demonstrate God's love and character.
- Every challenge becomes an occasion to trust God and grow in faith.
- Every success becomes a reason to give God glory and serve others more effectively.
- Every failure becomes a learning opportunity that builds character and dependence on God.

Your Legacy Leadership Plan

Consider what kind of legacy you want to build through your project management career.

Personal Reflection Questions

- What do you want people to say about you as a leader after you're gone?
- How do you want your project management work to contribute to God's Kingdom?
- Who are you intentionally developing to become better leaders?

- What character qualities do you need to develop to become a more effective mentor?

- How will you measure success in your leadership development efforts?

Legacy Action Steps

- **Identify Your Mentees:** Choose two to three people you will intentionally invest in over the next 12 months.

- **Create Development Plans:** Establish specific goals and activities for each mentoring relationship.

- **Schedule Regular Investment:** Block time weekly for mentoring activities and relationship building.

- **Build Learning Resources:** Compile books, articles, and other resources that will help others grow.

- **Document Your Journey:** Keep records of lessons learned that you can share with future mentees.

- **Seek Your Own Mentors:** Continue learning from others who are farther along on their leadership journey.

The Multiplication Vision

Imagine if you developed five excellent Christian project managers over your career, and each of them developed five more, and each of those developed five more. In three generations, your leadership development efforts would have influenced 125 project managers who were serving God's Kingdom through excellent work.

Now imagine the projects they would manage, the teams they would develop, the organizations they would transform, and the Kingdom impact they would create. That's the multiplication potential of legacy leadership.

A Personal Testimony: The Leader Who Changed Everything

I want to close this chapter with a personal testimony about the project leader who most influenced my approach to leadership and faith integration.

Early in my career, I worked for Beth, a woman who managed large-scale healthcare technology implementations. On paper, she wasn't particularly impressive. She didn't have advanced degrees, prestigious certifications, or a flashy leadership style. But she had something more valuable. She genuinely cared about developing the people who worked for her.

Beth spent time getting to know each team member personally. She understood our career goals, our family situations, and our personal challenges. She created opportunities for us to take on increasing responsibility, always with the support and coaching we needed to succeed. When we made mistakes, she helped us learn from them without making us feel like failures.

Most importantly, Beth demonstrated how to integrate faith with excellent work. She prayed for our projects and our team members by name. She made decisions based on biblical principles, even when it would have been easier to compromise. She treated every project as an opportunity to serve others and honor God.

What made Beth particularly remarkable was how she masterfully balanced work and life while maintaining her commitment to excellence. I'll never forget the times she called in to critical project meetings from her son's lacrosse games, expertly managing complex technical discussions while cheering from the sidelines. She showed us that being fully present for our families and fully committed to our work weren't mutually exclusive; they were both expressions of faithful stewardship.

Under Beth's leadership, I learned not just how to manage projects but how to lead people with character and integrity. I discovered that project management could be ministry, not just professional work. I saw how investing in people's development creates multiplication effects that extend far beyond any single project.

Beth's investment in me didn't end when I moved on to other roles. She continued to mentor me through career transitions, offering wisdom and guidance whenever I needed it. She served as a valuable job reference, advocating for my abilities and character to potential employers. Her ongoing support and belief in my potential gave me the confidence to pursue leadership opportunities I might not have otherwise considered.

Tragically, Beth and her husband were killed during Hurricane Sandy in 2012 when a tree fell on the truck they were in. The loss was devastating, not just for her family but for the countless people whose lives she had touched through her leadership and mentoring. I miss her terribly, and I look forward to seeing her again in heaven.

Beth's influence still continues through the leaders she developed. Several of us have gone on to senior leadership positions where we're applying the principles she taught us. We're mentoring the next generation using the same approach she used with us—balancing excellence with compassion, integrating faith with work, and showing that family and career can both be priorities when approached with wisdom and intentionality. Her legacy multiplies through every person we develop and every project we lead with the character she modeled.

That's the power of legacy leadership. The impact extends far beyond your own career and accomplishments, and continues to influence lives and careers long after you're gone.

As I reflect on Beth's influence on my life, I'm compelled to ask myself this: Who will be able to tell similar stories about my influence in their leadership development? What legacy am I building through the people I'm developing today?

This question should drive every Christian project manager to think beyond immediate project success to long-term leadership development. We have the opportunity to influence not just current projects but future generations of leaders who will manage projects we'll never see, serve people we'll never meet, and advance God's Kingdom in ways we can't imagine.

The Ultimate Performance Review

> *His lord said to him, "Well done, good and faithful servant; you were faithful over a few things, I will make you ruler over many things. Enter into the joy of your lord."*
>
> —Matt. 25:21

Someday, every Christian project manager will stand before the ultimate Project Sponsor for the ultimate performance review. On that day, the questions won't be about budget variance or schedule adherence. They'll be about faithfulness, stewardship, and Kingdom impact.

> *Were you faithful with the resources I entrusted to you?*
>
> *Did you develop the people I placed under your leadership?*
>
> *How did your work serve others and advance My Kingdom?*

What kind of leader did you become through the challenges I allowed in your life?

When we approach our project management careers with these questions in mind, everything changes. Projects become opportunities for ministry. Team development becomes discipleship. Challenges become character-building experiences. Success becomes a platform for greater service.

The goal isn't just to hear "well done" for our project management performance. It's to hear "well done, good and faithful servant" for how we stewarded every opportunity to serve, develop, and lead others.

Your Leadership Legacy Starts Today

Legacy leadership isn't something you think about at the end of your career. It's something you build with every project, every team interaction, and every opportunity to influence others. The person you mentor today might become the leader who mentors dozens of others tomorrow. The character you model in this project might inspire someone to pursue excellence and integrity throughout their career. The biblical principle you share might transform how someone approaches leadership for the rest of their life.

Legacy leadership begins with the decision to see every project as an opportunity to develop people, every challenge as a chance to build character, and every success as a platform for serving others. It continues with the intentional investment of time, energy, and wisdom in the people God has placed around you. It multiplies through the leaders you develop, who in turn develop other leaders. That's living a Faith Forward Life!

The Master Project Manager spent three years developing 12 ordinary people who would go on to change the world. He invested in their character, developed their capabilities, and empowered them to carry on His mission after He was gone. His legacy continues to multiply thousands of years later through the countless people who are His disciples, who faithfully and obediently disciple others, who also become His disciples that disciple other believers, and so on.

You have the same opportunity. The question is whether you'll embrace the calling to become a legacy leader who develops others for Kingdom impact.

Your project management career is more than a profession. It's a platform for building God's Kingdom through the development of people who will serve Him long after your projects are completed and your career is finished.

The Master Project Manager is ready to develop you into the leader He wants you to become. Are you ready to accept the responsibility and privilege of developing others in the same way?

His legacy through you starts today. How will you build it?

Afterword

As I sit in my office, looking at the completed manuscript of this book, I'm overwhelmed by gratitude for the journey that brought these pages to life. This work represents more than just another project management methodology. It's the convergence of profound influences that have shaped not only my professional practice but my very understanding of what it means to lead with excellence and integrity.

The Convergence of Truth

For over two decades, I've walked the sometimes challenging path of integrating biblical wisdom with secular project management practices. As I already mentioned, I discovered Stephen R. Covey's masterwork, The 7 Habits of Highly Effective People, early in my career and found myself reading it alongside my daily Bible study. Years later, I encountered his son Stephen M. R. Covey's profound work *The Speed of Trust*, which revealed another layer of truth—that trust is indeed the foundational principle that makes all project success possible. The final piece of this transformative puzzle came when I read Stephen R. Covey's *The 8th Habit: From Effectiveness to Greatness*. Although it was published between the other two, it was the last I discovered on my personal journey. This sequence proved providential as each book built upon my understanding in the perfect order for my development, elevating the conversation from personal effectiveness to trust-building to finding my voice and inspiring others to find theirs.

What emerged was a revelation. The principles that make project managers truly effective are not merely business strategies. They are reflections of eternal truths that God has woven into the fabric of creation itself.

Stephen R. Covey wrote in *The 7 Habits of Highly Effective People*, "Private victories precede public victories." This truth echoes throughout Scripture, from David's private worship before his public victories to Jesus's 40 days in the wilderness before His public ministry. But in *The 8th Habit*, Covey took this further, showing us that true leadership involves helping others find their unique voice and contribution. In project management, I've witnessed countless times how managers' private disciplines—prayer, character development, and spiritual grounding—determine not only the public success of their teams and deliverables but also their ability to inspire others to greatness.

Afterword

When the Gospel Meets the Workplace

Throughout my career, I've encountered numerous situations where direct biblical references would have been inappropriate or ineffective. In these moments, I discovered that the Covey principles served as a bridge—a way to demonstrate the fruit of the Spirit without explicitly naming it. The results were remarkable. Teams that operated under these principles consistently outperformed their peers, not just in metrics but in morale, retention, and overall satisfaction.

When I practiced "seek first to understand, then to be understood," my stakeholders experienced what Scripture calls gentleness and patience. When I emphasized "begin with the end in mind," my teams demonstrated self-control and faithfulness. When I applied the 13 Behaviors from Stephen M. R. Covey's *The Speed of Trust*—behaviors like talking straight, showing respect, and demonstrating accountability— I watched trust levels soar and project velocity increase exponentially.

But it was *The 8th Habit* that helped me understand the deeper purpose behind effective project management. Covey's concept of finding your voice—that unique personal significance that comes from discovering your passion, talent, need, and conscience—transformed how I viewed my role as a project manager. No longer was I simply coordinating tasks; I was helping team members discover and express their own voices while serving a need greater than ourselves.

These weren't coincidences. They were manifestations

of God's truth working through secular language in professional environments. The 13 Behaviors became my practical toolkit for demonstrating Christian character in ways that even the most secular-minded stakeholders could appreciate and respect, while *The 8th Habit* provided the framework for inspiring others toward their highest potential.

The Fruits of the Spirit Through Seven Habits, The Eighth Habit, and Trust Behaviors

The connection between *The 7 Habits of Highly Effective People*, *The 8th Habit*, *The Speed of Trust*, and the nine fruits of the Spirit in Galatians 5:22-23 became increasingly clear as I applied all three frameworks in my project management practice.

> ***Love*** finds its expression in Habit 4: "Think Win-Win," the trust behavior of "Show Respect," and *The 8th Habit's* emphasis on serving others' highest good. Stephen R. Covey states, "Win-Win is a frame of mind and heart that constantly seeks mutual benefit in all human interactions." This mirrors perfectly the biblical command to "love your neighbor as yourself." When we help others find their voice and reach their potential, we demonstrate love in its purest form.
>
> ***Joy*** emerges through Habit 7: "Sharpen the Saw," the trust behavior of "Create Transparency," and *The*

8th Habit's discovery of personal significance. The joy that comes from continuous growth and renewal—combined with helping others discover their unique contribution—transforms project managers from mere task coordinators into life-giving leaders who inspire their teams toward greatness.

Peace is cultivated through Habit 2: "Begin with the End in Mind," the trust behavior of "Clarify Expectations," and *The 8th Habit's* focus on conscience-driven leadership. When project managers operate from a clear vision rooted in principles rather than circumstances, they maintain peace even in chaos. This peace becomes contagious when team members understand not just what they're doing but why it matters.

Longsuffering (Patience) is developed through Habit 3: "Put First Things First," the trust behavior of "Practice Accountability," and *The 8th Habit's* understanding that meaningful change takes time. Project managers who master these concepts learn to wait for the right timing, persist through difficulties, and maintain a long-term perspective while helping others develop their capabilities.

Kindness flows naturally from Habit 6: "Synergize," the trust behavior of "Listen First," and *The 8th Habit's* emphasis on valuing others' unique contributions. True synergy occurs when we create environments where team members feel valued, heard, and empowered to express their authentic voice and contribute their best.

Goodness is embodied in Habit 1: "Be Proactive," the trust behavior of "Talk Straight," and *The 8th Habit's* call to moral authority. Goodness in project management means taking responsibility, being part of the solution, and consistently choosing actions that serve the greater good while inspiring others to do the same.

Faithfulness is strengthened through Habit 5: "Seek First to Understand, Then to Be Understood," the trust behavior of "Keep Commitments," and *The 8th Habit's* emphasis on integrity. This creates the foundation of trust necessary for others to risk vulnerability in finding and expressing their voice.

Gentleness permeates all frameworks but is particularly evident in *The 8th Habit's* approach to inspiring rather than manipulating. When we lead with moral authority rather than positional power, we create the psychological safety necessary for others to discover their greatness.

Self-Control is the foundation that makes all other qualities possible and is reflected in *The 8th Habit's* discipline of conscience-driven decision-making. Project managers who embody this fruit make decisions based on principles rather than emotions, creating stability that allows others to flourish.

The Trust Dividend and Finding Voice in Project Management

One of the most profound realizations in my project management journey has been understanding how Stephen M. R. Covey's "trust dividend" combines with *The 8th Habit's* concept of voice to create exponential results. When trust is high and team members are operating from their unique strengths and passions, the results are remarkable—faster decision-making, increased innovation, higher engagement, and dramatically improved team morale.

The 13 Behaviors became my practical road map for building this trust, while *The 8th Habit* provided the framework for helping others discover their significance. When I practiced "Right Wrongs" by acknowledging mistakes quickly, team members felt safe to take risks and express their authentic voice. When I consistently applied "Deliver Results" while helping others identify their unique contributions, stakeholders began giving me greater autonomy and resources.

These behaviors aren't just management techniques; they're expressions of biblical character traits that Jesus modeled perfectly. He helped the disciples find their voice and calling, built trust through consistent character, and inspired them to accomplish the greatest project in human history: the redemption of mankind.

The Faith at Work Series: A Vision for Kingdom Impact

This book, *If Jesus Was a Project Manager*, is just the beginning of a comprehensive journey we're taking together through the *Faith at Work* series under Faith Forward Life. Each book in this series addresses the critical intersection of faith and professional excellence, providing biblical frameworks for modern workplace challenges.

Coming Soon! Book 2: *If Jesus Was a Scrum Master*. Building on the foundation we've established here, our next exploration will dive deep into Agile leadership, communication, and conflict resolution through Christ's example. How did Jesus facilitate difficult conversations among His disciples? How did He handle resistance to change? How can we lead iterative improvement while maintaining eternal perspective?

The Complete Faith at Work Series

1. *If Jesus Was a Project Manager* (this book)—Faith-based leadership, planning, and team management

2. *If Jesus Was a Scrum Master*—Communication, conflict resolution, Agile leadership

3. *If Jesus Was a Product Owner*—Vision, customer value, and leading with clarity

4. *If Jesus Was a Business Analyst*—Translating vision into value, requirements with righteousness

5. ***What Would Jesus Do in a Layoff?***—Navigating corporate and personal hardship with compassion and supernatural peace
6. ***If Jesus Ran a Startup***—Innovation, faith-driven entrepreneurship, ethical business decision-making
7. ***On-the-Job Sword-Training (OJST)***—Daily devotional workbook with guided Scripture study, meditation, journaling, and prayers, featuring motivational quotes from throughout the *Faith at Work* series

The Eternal Perspective

What I've learned through decades of practice is that effective project management is ultimately about people—developing them, serving them, and creating environments where they can flourish and find their voice. This is precisely what Jesus did with His disciples. He didn't just deliver a project (salvation for humanity); He developed leaders who discovered their unique calling and would carry on the work long after His departure.

Every project we manage, every team we lead, every stakeholder we serve is an opportunity to demonstrate the character of Christ while helping others discover their God-given potential. Sometimes we do this through direct biblical application, as outlined in this book. Other times, we do it through the universal principles that reflect God's design for human flourishing—principles that Stephen R. Covey so brilliantly articulated in *The 7 Habits of Highly Effective People*, *The 8th Habit*, and the 13 Behaviors.

The beauty of this integrated approach is that it transcends cultural, religious, and organizational boundaries. Whether you're managing a project in a church setting or a Fortune 500 company, the principles remain the same because they're rooted in the unchanging nature of human relationships and God's design for how we should treat one another.

A Final Challenge

As you close this book and return to your project management responsibilities, I challenge you to see your work through the lens of eternity and purpose. The projects you manage may be temporary, but the people you influence are eternal. The character you develop through both triumph and trial will outlast any deliverable you produce. More importantly, your role in helping others find their voice and discover their significance may be the most important project outcome of all.

Whether you're leading a team that welcomes biblical principles or one that requires a more secular approach, remember that trust is the foundation and voice is the destination. The 13 Behaviors provide you with practical tools to build that trust daily, while *The 8th Habit* gives you the framework for inspiring greatness in others—all while demonstrating the character of Christ through actions that speak more loudly than words.

Consider implementing these behaviors systematically in your next project while also looking for opportunities to help team members discover their unique contributions.

- **Talk Straight:** Speak with honesty and integrity, even when it's difficult.

- **Demonstrate Respect:** Show you value others as individuals with unique contributions.

- **Create Transparency:** Share information openly and build authentic relationships.

- **Right Wrongs:** Address mistakes quickly and make things right.

- **Show Loyalty:** Give credit to others and speak positively about team members.

- **Deliver Results:** Establish your credibility through consistent performance.

- **Get Better:** Continuously improve and help others grow.

- **Confront Reality:** Address issues head-on with courage and compassion.

- **Clarify Expectations:** Ensure everyone understands their roles and responsibilities.

- **Practice Accountability:** Hold yourself and others accountable for results.

- **Listen First:** Seek to understand before being understood.
- **Keep Commitments:** Do what you say you'll do when you say you'll do it.
- **Extend Trust:** Give others the benefit of the doubt and empower them to succeed.

Whether you're leading a team that welcomes biblical principles or one that requires a more secular approach, remember that truth is truth. The same God who created the universe and established the principles of effective leadership also empowers you to be His representative in whatever environment you find yourself. Your role is not just to manage projects successfully but to help others discover the voice and significance that God has placed within them.

May your projects succeed not just in meeting scope, time, and budget constraints but in demonstrating the excellence of character that points others toward their highest potential and ultimately toward the ultimate Project Manager—the One who began a good work in you and "will complete *it* until the day of Jesus Christ" (Phil. 1:6).

I've playfully noted "Oh My Stephen" throughout this book, and Covey got it right when he focused on character-based leadership and the power of helping others find their voice. But as followers of Jesus, we know the ultimate source of that character and the One who calls each person to their unique purpose. May we continue to bridge the sacred

Afterword

and secular, demonstrating that the best business practices are simply reflections of timeless spiritual truths.

The vineyard is vast, the harvest is plentiful, and the projects are many. May we manage them all for His glory and the benefit of those we're called to serve, always remembering that our greatest success may be in helping others discover and express the voice that God has given them.

> *And whatever you do, do it heartily, as to the Lord and not to men, knowing that from the Lord you will receive the reward of the inheritance; for you serve the Lord Christ.*
>
> —Col. 3:23-24

To God be the glory for the great things He has done—in our projects, through our teams, and in the lives of those who discover their voice and calling through our leadership.

Watch for Book 2:
If Jesus Was a Scrum Master—coming soon!
Continue your Faith at Work journey
at FaithForwardLife.com.

Acknowledgments

My deepest appreciation to all my mentors, managers (good and bad), and colleagues who have taught me, encouraged me, supported me, and sometimes pushed me to grow to be better and better and better.

My thanks also to my fellow project management experts who kindly shared and published their knowledge, techniques, and wonderful tools and templates for all of us to benefit from.

Special thanks to Stephen R. Covey, God rest his soul, for writing *The 7 Habits of Highly Effective People* and *The 8th Habit* that were such a huge influence on my life and early career.

And thanks to Stephen M. R. Covey, his son, who wrote *The Speed of Trust*, in which his 13 Behaviors of high-trust leaders further influenced me to be a better leader during the height of my project management career.

APPENDIX A
Biblical Project Management Principles: Quick Reference

Leadership Principles

Servant Leadership

- **Foundation Scripture:** "But whoever desires to become great among you, let him be your servant" (Matt. 20:26).

- **Core Principle:** Lead by serving others rather than demanding service.

- **Application:** Remove obstacles for your team, provide resources, facilitate communication.

- **Key Practice:** Ask "How can I help you succeed?" instead of "What's your status?"

Character First

- **Foundation Scripture:** "Moreover it is required in stewards that one be found faithful" (1 Cor. 4:2).
- **Core Principle:** Build character before competence in yourself and others.
- **Application:** Recruit for integrity, work ethic, and coachability over technical skills alone.
- **Key Practice:** Invest time in understanding team members' values and motivations.

Humble Authority

- **Foundation Scripture**: "Take My yoke upon you and learn from Me, for I am gentle and lowly in heart" (Matt. 11:29).
- **Core Principle:** Exercise authority through service rather than position.
- **Application:** Create psychological safety where people can admit mistakes and ask for help.
- **Key Practice:** Model vulnerability by acknowledging your own limitations and mistakes.

People Development

- **Foundation Scripture:** "And the things that you have heard from me among many witnesses, commit these to faithful men who will be able to teach others also" (2 Tim. 2:2).

- **Core Principle:** Invest in developing others as a primary leadership responsibility.

- **Application:** Create individual development plans for each team member.

- **Key Practice:** Measure your success by the leaders you develop, not just projects you complete.

Planning Principles

Stewardship Planning

- **Foundation Scripture:** "A man's heart plans his way, but the Lord directs his steps" (Prov. 16:9).

- **Core Principle:** Plan as a faithful steward of God's resources.

- **Application:** Balance thorough preparation with trust in God's sovereignty.

- **Key Practice:** Begin planning sessions with prayer for wisdom and guidance.

Flexible Structure

- **Foundation Scripture:** "Come now, you who say, 'Today or tomorrow we will go to such and such a city.' . . . Instead you *ought* to say, 'If the Lord wills, we shall live and do this or that.'" (James 4:13, 15).

- **Core Principle:** Create detailed plans that accommodate divine direction.

- **Application:** Build flexibility into timelines and resource allocations.

- **Key Practice:** Hold plans with confident flexibility—committed to objectives, flexible about methods.

Partnership with Providence

- **Foundation Scripture:** "Commit your works to the Lord, and your thoughts will be established" (Prov. 16:3).

- **Core Principle:** Plan thoroughly while trusting God's sovereignty.

- **Application:** Leave room in plans for divine intervention and redirection.

- **Key Practice:** Have regular plan reviews to assess whether God is redirecting your path.

Eternal Perspective

- **Foundation Scripture:** "But seek first the kingdom of God and His righteousness, and all these things shall be added to you" (Matt. 6:33).

- **Core Principle:** Consider long-term Kingdom impact in all planning decisions.

- **Application:** Evaluate project decisions based on how they serve God's purposes.

- **Key Practice:** Ask "How does this project advance God's Kingdom?" in planning sessions.

Communication Principles

Heart Connection

- **Foundation Scripture:** "For out of the abundance of the heart the mouth speaks" (Matt. 12:34).

- **Core Principle:** Connect with people's hearts before transferring information.

- **Application:** Understand stakeholder concerns and motivations before presenting solutions.

- **Key Practice:** Start difficult conversations by acknowledging the person's value and perspective.

Story-Based Communication

- **Foundation Scripture:** "Then He spoke many things to them in parables" (Matt. 13:3).

- **Core Principle:** Use narratives that help people understand purpose and meaning.

- **Application:** Replace technical specifications with stories about how success will impact real people.

- **Key Practice:** Create user stories that connect functional requirements to human outcomes.

Active Listening

- **Foundation Scripture:** "So then, my beloved brethren, let every man be swift to hear, slow to speak, slow to wrath" (James 1:19).

- **Core Principle:** Seek to understand before seeking to be understood.

- **Application:** Listen for emotions and underlying concerns, not just words.

- **Key Practice:** Reflect on what you've heard before responding with your own perspective.

Truth with Love

- **Foundation Scripture:** "But, speaking the truth in love, may grow up in all things into Him who is the head—Christ" (Eph. 4:15).
- **Core Principle:** Communicate honestly while maintaining relationships.
- **Application:** Address problems directly but without personal attacks.
- **Key Practice:** Combine honesty about challenges with hope for solutions.

Team-Building Principles

Diverse Unity

- **Foundation Scripture:** "For as the body is one and has many members, but all the members of that one body, being many, are one body, so also *is* Christ" (1 Cor. 12:12).
- **Core Principle:** Build teams that combine diverse skills with unified purpose.
- **Application:** Recruit for complementary strengths while ensuring shared values.
- **Key Practice:** Regularly connect individual tasks to the larger team mission.

Psychological Safety

- **Foundation Scripture:** "There is no fear in love; but perfect love casts out fear" (1 John 4:18).
- **Core Principle:** Create environments where people feel safe to contribute and grow.
- **Application:** Respond to mistakes with learning opportunities rather than punishment.
- **Key Practice:** Model vulnerability and encourage questions without judgment.

Progressive Development

- **Foundation Scripture:** "After these things the Lord appointed seventy others also, and sent them two by two" (Luke 10:1).
- **Core Principle:** Give people increasingly challenging opportunities with appropriate support.
- **Application:** Provide stretch assignments that develop capabilities without overwhelming people.
- **Key Practice:** Debrief experiences to capture learning and celebrate growth.

Shared Mission

- **Foundation Scripture:** "Then He appointed twelve, that they might be with Him and that He might send them out to preach" (Mark 3:14).
- **Core Principle:** Unite teams around purposes larger than individual objectives.
- **Application:** Help team members understand how their work serves others and honors God.
- **Key Practice:** Begin team meetings by connecting current work to the larger vision.

Conflict Resolution Principles

Grace-Based Approach

- **Foundation Scripture:** "Blessed *are* the peacemakers, for they shall be called sons of God" (Matt. 5:9).
- **Core Principle:** Handle conflicts with gentleness, respect, authenticity, compassion, and empowerment.
- **Application:** Approach disagreements as opportunities to build stronger relationships.

- **Key Practice:** Use the GRACE method (Gentle, Respectful, Authentic, Compassionate, Empowering).

Root Cause Focus

- **Foundation Scripture:** "But when He saw the multitudes, He was moved with compassion for them, because they were weary and scattered, like sheep having no shepherd" (Matt. 9:36).
- **Core Principle:** Address underlying needs and concerns rather than surface disagreements.
- **Application:** Look beyond stated positions to understand what people really need.
- **Key Practice:** Ask "What would help you feel successful in this situation?"

Win-Win Solutions

- **Foundation Scripture:** "But we believe that through the grace of the Lord Jesus Christ we shall be saved in the same manner as they" (Acts 15:11).
- **Core Principle:** Seek solutions that serve everyone's legitimate interests.
- **Application:** Focus on shared objectives and values as a foundation for problem-solving.

- **Key Practice:** Facilitate collaborative solution development rather than imposing decisions.

Restoration Goals

- **Foundation Scripture:** "Then Peter came to Him and said, 'Lord, how often shall my brother sin against me, and I forgive him? Up to seven times?' Jesus said to him, 'I do not say to you, up to seven times, but up to seventy times seven'" (Matt. 18:21-22).

- **Core Principle:** Work toward reconciliation and stronger relationships.

- **Application:** Focus on rebuilding trust and understanding, not winning arguments.

- **Key Practice:** Follow up after conflict resolution to ensure relationships are restored.

Risk Management Principles

PRAY Method

- **Foundation Scripture:** "Be anxious for nothing, but in everything by prayer and supplication, with thanksgiving, let your requests be made known to God" (Phil. 4:6).

- **Core Principle:** Predict, Risk-Assess, Act, Yield to God (PRAY)
- **Application:** Combine prudent planning with trust in God's sovereignty.
- **Key Practice:** Integrate prayer into risk assessment and response planning.

Faith-Based Response

- **Foundation Scripture:** "The name of the Lord *is* a strong tower; the righteous run to it and are safe" (Prov, 18:10).
- **Core Principle:** Combine prudent planning with trust in God's provision.
- **Application:** Take appropriate preventive actions while trusting God for ultimate outcomes.
- **Key Practice:** Include spiritual actions (prayer, seeking counsel) alongside practical responses.

Opportunity Focus

- **Foundation Scripture:** "And we know that all things work together for good to those who love God, to those who are the called according to *His* purpose" (Rom. 8:28).
- **Core Principle:** Look for opportunities within risks rather than just threats.

- **Application:** Consider how challenges might create unexpected benefits or learning.
- **Key Practice:** Ask "What good might come from this risk?" alongside threat assessment.

Spiritual Dimensions

- **Foundation Scripture:** "For we do not wrestle against flesh and blood, but against principalities, against powers" (Eph. 6:12).
- **Core Principle:** Consider spiritual and relational risks alongside technical and business risks.
- **Application:** Assess how attitudes and relationships might affect project success.
- **Key Practice:** Include team unity and stakeholder relationships in risk registers.

Quality Principles

Excellence as Worship

- **Foundation Scripture:** "And whatever you do, do it heartily, as to the Lord and not to men" (Col. 3:23).
- **Core Principle:** Deliver excellent work as an expression of worship to God.

- **Application:** Approach every deliverable as an opportunity to honor God through quality.
- **Key Practice:** Ask "Does this work reflect God's character?" before declaring anything complete.

Stakeholder Service

- **Foundation Scripture:** "She perceives that her merchandise *is* good, and her lamp does not go out by night" (Prov. 31:18).
- **Core Principle:** Define quality in terms of serving others well.
- **Application:** Focus on user experience and stakeholder satisfaction, not just technical specifications.
- **Key Practice:** Regularly ask stakeholders "How well is this serving your needs?"

Continuous Improvement

- **Foundation Scripture:** "And God saw the light, that *it was* good" (Gen. 1:4).
- **Core Principle:** Build quality into every phase rather than adding it at the end.
- **Application:** Establish quality checkpoints throughout a project lifecycle.

- **Key Practice:** Conduct regular quality reviews and adjust processes based on feedback.

Legacy Standards

- **Foundation Scripture:** "So he was seven years in building it" (1 Kings 6:38).
- **Core Principle:** Create work that serves long-term purposes, not just immediate needs.
- **Application:** Consider maintainability, scalability, and future enhancement in design decisions.
- **Key Practice:** Ask "Will this work make future projects easier or harder?"

Success Principles

Kingdom Impact

- **Foundation Scripture:** "But seek first the kingdom of God and His righteousness, and all these things shall be added to you" (Matt. 6:33).
- **Core Principle:** Measure success by Kingdom advancement as well as project objectives.
- **Application:** Evaluate projects based on how they serve others and advance God's purposes.
- **Key Practice:** Include Kingdom impact in project success criteria.

People Development

- **Foundation Scripture:** "And the things that you have heard from me among many witnesses, commit these to faithful men who will be able to teach others also" (2 Tim. 2:2).

- **Core Principle:** Include team growth and capability-building in success criteria.

- **Application:** Track how team members develop through project experience.

- **Key Practice:** Measure project success partly by the leaders developed.

Relationship Building

- **Foundation Scripture:** "A man *who has* friends must himself be friendly, but there is a friend *who* sticks closer than a brother" (Prov. 18:24).

- **Core Principle:** Evaluate success by strengthened relationships and increased trust.

- **Application:** Monitor stakeholder satisfaction and team cohesion throughout projects.

- **Key Practice:** Include relationship health in regular project reviews.

Character Growth

- **Foundation Scripture:** "For whom He foreknew, He also predestined to *be* conformed to the image of His Son" (Rom. 8:29).

- **Core Principle:** Assess success by character development in yourself and others.

- **Application:** Use project challenges as opportunities for spiritual and personal growth.

- **Key Practice:** Reflect on what character qualities each project developed in you and your team.

Failure Recovery Principles

Learning Orientation

- **Foundation Scripture:** "The heart of the prudent acquires knowledge, and the ear of the wise seeks knowledge" (Prov. 18:15).

- **Core Principle:** Treat failures as learning opportunities rather than final judgments.

- **Application:** Focus post-failure analysis on insights gained rather than blame assignment.

- **Key Practice:** Ask "What can we learn?" before asking "Who was responsible?"

Responsibility Without Shame

- **Foundation Scripture:** "If we confess our sins, He is faithful and just to forgive us *our* sins and to cleanse us from all unrighteousness" (1 John 1:9).

- **Core Principle:** Accept accountability while receiving God's forgiveness.

- **Application:** Take responsibility for your contributions to failure without taking on false guilt.

- **Key Practice:** Distinguish between your actual responsibility and circumstances beyond your control.

Redemptive Purpose

- **Foundation Scripture:** "And we know that all things work together for good to those who love God, to those who are the called according to *His* purpose" (Rom. 8:28).

- **Core Principle:** Trust God to bring good from difficult circumstances.

- **Application:** Look for how apparent failures might be preparation for future opportunities.

- **Key Practice:** Remain open to how God might use failure experiences for His purposes.

Service from Experience

- **Foundation Scripture:** "Blessed *be* the . . . God of all comfort, who comforts us in all our tribulation, that we may be able to comfort those who are in any trouble" (2 Cor. 1:3-4).

- **Core Principle:** Use failure experiences to help others navigate similar challenges.

- **Application:** Mentor others facing difficulties using wisdom gained from your own setbacks.

- **Key Practice:** Share failure stories appropriately to encourage and instruct others.

Legacy Principles

Multiplication Mindset

- **Foundation Scripture:** "And the things that you have heard from me among many witnesses, commit these to faithful men who will be able to teach others also" (2 Tim. 2:2).

- **Core Principle:** Develop leaders who will develop other leaders.

- **Application:** Invest in people who have the potential to mentor others.

- **Key Practice:** Track how your mentees are developing others in their own leadership roles.

Character Foundation

- **Foundation Scripture:** "But you, O man of God, flee these things and pursue righteousness, godliness, faith, love, patience, gentleness" (1 Tim. 6:11).
- **Core Principle:** Build legacy on character rather than achievements.
- **Application:** Focus on becoming the kind of person worth following and emulating.
- **Key Practice:** Regularly assess your character development and seek accountability.

Kingdom Perspective

- **Foundation Scripture:** "For we must all appear before the judgment seat of Christ, that each one may receive the things *done* in the body, according to what he has done, whether good or bad" (2 Cor. 5:10).
- **Core Principle:** Evaluate legacy by eternal impact rather than temporal success.
- **Application:** Consider how your leadership development efforts serve God's Kingdom.

- **Key Practice:** Ask "How will this person serve God's purposes through their leadership?"

Mentoring Commitment

- **Foundation Scripture:** "So when they had eaten breakfast, Jesus said to Simon Peter, 'Simon, *son* of Jonah, do you love Me more than these?' . . . He said to him, 'Feed My lambs'" (John 21:15).

- **Core Principle:** Intentionally invest in developing the next generation.

- **Application:** Make leadership development a priority rather than an optional activity.

- **Key Practice:** Commit specific time and resources to mentoring relationships.

APPENDIX B
Prayers for Project Managers

Daily Prayers

Morning Prayer for Project Managers

Father, as I begin this day, I offer my work to You as an act of worship. Help me serve others excellently, lead with humility, communicate with love, and handle challenges with faith. Guide my decisions, bless my relationships, and use my work to advance Your Kingdom. May everything I do today bring glory to Your name. In Jesus's name, amen.

Evening Prayer for Project Managers

Lord, thank You for Your faithfulness throughout this day. I acknowledge that any success came from Your blessing and provision. Help me learn from the challenges I faced and grow in wisdom and character. Grant me rest that refreshes my body and spirit for tomorrow's opportunities to serve You and others. In Jesus's name, amen.

Midday Reset Prayer

Heavenly Father, in the busyness of this day, I pause to remember that You are in control. Help me approach the rest of this day with patience, wisdom, and trust in Your guidance. Refresh my spirit and renew my focus on serving others well. In Jesus's name, amen.

Project Phase Prayers

Prayer for Project Initiation

Father, as we begin this project, we acknowledge that all good gifts come from You. Grant us wisdom to plan well, unity to work together effectively, and faithfulness to steward the resources You've provided. Help us serve others excellently and bring glory to Your name through our work. Guide our steps and bless our efforts according to Your will. In Jesus's name, amen.

Prayer for Project Planning

Lord, we come before You seeking wisdom for the planning of this project. Help us see clearly the needs we are trying to meet and the best ways to serve those who will be affected by our work. Grant us discernment to make good decisions about timelines, resources, and priorities. May our plans honor You and serve others well. In Jesus's name, amen.

Prayer for Project Execution

Heavenly Father, as we move into the active work of this project, we depend on Your guidance and strength. Help us work with excellence, communicate with love, and solve problems with wisdom. When challenges arise, remind us to trust in You and treat difficulties as opportunities for growth. Bless our efforts and use our work for Your glory. In Jesus's name, amen.

Prayer for Project Closure

Father, as this project comes to an end, we give You thanks for Your faithfulness throughout this journey. Thank You for the team You assembled, the resources You provided, and the lessons You taught us. Help us celebrate appropriately, learn thoroughly, and transition well. Use this experience to prepare us for greater service to You and others. In Jesus's name, amen.

Team and Relationship Prayers

Prayer for Team Unity

Lord, You have brought together people with different backgrounds, skills, and perspectives to accomplish this work. Help us appreciate our differences while maintaining unity of purpose. Give us patience with each other, compassion for each other's challenges, and commitment to each other's successes. Make us a team that reflects Your love and grace. In Jesus's name, amen.

Prayer for Difficult Team Members

Father, I bring before You the challenges I'm experiencing with [name]. Help me see them as You see them and respond with grace and patience. Give me wisdom to address problems constructively and build a relationship that honors You. Work in their heart and mine to create understanding and mutual respect. In Jesus's name, amen.

Prayer for Stakeholder Relationships

Lord, we pray for all the people affected by this project. Help us understand their needs, address their concerns, and serve them with excellence. Give us favor in our relationships and help us be trustworthy stewards of their confidence. May our interactions reflect Your love and character. In Jesus's name, amen.

Prayer for New Team Members

Heavenly Father, thank You for bringing [name] to our team. Help them feel welcomed and valued. Give them confidence as they learn new roles and responsibilities. Help us support their growth and create an environment where they can contribute their best. Use this experience to bless both them and our entire team. In Jesus's name, amen.

Challenge and Crisis Prayers

Prayer for Challenging Times

Father, this project is facing difficulties that test our faith and challenge our capabilities. We acknowledge our dependence on You and ask for Your intervention. Give us courage to face challenges, wisdom to solve problems, and faith to trust Your provision. Help us grow through difficulties and glorify You in how we respond. In Jesus's name, amen.

Prayer for Budget Pressures

Lord, we are facing financial constraints that create difficult decisions about this project. Grant us wisdom to be good stewards of the resources available while still serving stakeholders well. Help us find creative solutions that honor both fiscal responsibility and excellence in service. We trust You to provide what is needed. In Jesus's name, amen.

Prayer for Timeline Pressures

Heavenly Father, we are feeling pressure to complete this work faster than seems wise or realistic. Give us the courage to advocate for timelines that allow for quality and excellence. Help us communicate clearly about what is possible and find solutions that serve stakeholders well without compromising integrity. In Jesus's name, amen.

Prayer for Technical Difficulties

Lord, we are facing technical challenges that are beyond our current knowledge and capabilities. We ask for Your wisdom and guidance in finding solutions. Bring us the right resources, the right people, and the right insights to overcome these obstacles. Help us learn and grow through these difficulties. In Jesus's name, amen.

Prayer for Stakeholder Conflicts

Father, there are disagreements among the people involved in this project that are creating tension and slowing progress. Help us be peacemakers who bring understanding and resolution. Give us wisdom to address the real issues behind the surface conflicts. Help all parties focus on our shared objectives and work together constructively. In Jesus's name, amen.

Decision-Making Prayers

Prayer for Wisdom in Decision-Making

Heavenly Father, we face complex decisions that affect many people. Grant us wisdom that comes from above—wisdom that is pure, peaceable, gentle, reasonable, and full of mercy and good fruits. Help us see clearly, think carefully, and choose wisely. Guide us to decisions that honor You and serve others well. In Jesus's name, amen.

Prayer for Resource Allocation

Lord, we have limited resources and many competing priorities. Help us allocate time, money, and people in ways that maximize value for those we serve. Give us wisdom to distinguish between what is urgent and what is important. Help us be faithful stewards of all You have entrusted to us. In Jesus's name, amen.

Prayer for Vendor Selection

Father, we need to choose partners and vendors for this project. Help us select organizations and people who share our commitment to excellence and integrity. Give us discernment to see beyond marketing presentations to the reality of capabilities and character. Guide us to partnerships that will serve our stakeholders well. In Jesus's name, amen.

Prayer for Scope Changes

Lord, we are being asked to modify the scope of this project in ways that create difficult decisions. Help us evaluate these changes based on how they will serve the people we are trying to help. Give us wisdom to say yes to changes that add value and courage to say no to changes that would compromise quality or effectiveness. In Jesus's name, amen.

Growth and Development Prayers

Prayer for Personal Growth

Lord, use my project management work to conform me to the image of Your Son. Develop in me the character qualities of Jesus—His humility, His love for others, His commitment to excellence, and His dependence on the Father. Help me grow through every challenge and become a more effective leader and servant. In Jesus's name, amen.

Prayer for Professional Development

Heavenly Father, help me to continue growing in my project management capabilities. Give me wisdom to know what skills to develop and how to improve my effectiveness. Bring me learning opportunities, mentors, and resources that will help me serve others better. Help me be a good steward of the talents and opportunities You have given me. In Jesus's name, amen.

Prayer for Team Member Development

Lord, I pray for the growth and development of each person on this team. Help me see their potential and create opportunities for them to learn and advance. Give me wisdom to provide feedback that encourages and instructs. Use this project experience to prepare them for greater responsibilities and more effective service. In Jesus's name, amen.

Prayer for Organizational Learning

Father, help our organization to learn and improve through this project experience. May the lessons we learn benefit future projects and the people they serve. Help us capture and share insights that will make our organization more effective in its mission. Use our work to build capabilities that will serve Your purposes. In Jesus's name, amen.

Success and Completion Prayers

Prayer for Excellence

Lord, You are a God of excellence, and we want our work to reflect Your character. Help us deliver results that honor You and serve others well. Give us attention to detail, commitment to quality, and perseverance to finish well. May our work be a testimony to Your faithfulness and grace. In Jesus's name, amen.

Prayer for Celebration

Father, You have blessed our efforts and enabled us to accomplish more than we could have achieved on our own. Help us celebrate appropriately, giving You glory while recognizing the contributions of all who helped. May our joy in success motivate us to even greater service in the future. In Jesus's name, amen.

Prayer for Transition

Lord, as this project transitions from our team to ongoing operations, we pray for those who will maintain and enhance what we have built. Help them to be successful in their responsibilities. May the foundation we have laid serve Your purposes for years to come. Bless all who will benefit from this work. In Jesus's name, amen.

Prayer for Future Opportunities

Heavenly Father, thank You for the privilege of serving through this project. Prepare us for future opportunities to use our gifts and experience in Your service. Help us carry forward the lessons we have learned and the relationships we have built. Guide us to our next assignments in Your Kingdom work. In Jesus's name, amen.

Special Situation Prayers

Prayer for Failure Recovery

Lord, this project has not achieved the results we hoped for, and we are disappointed. Help us learn from this experience without being defined by it. Show us how to take responsibility where appropriate while trusting You for outcomes beyond our control. Use this setback to prepare us for future success in serving You and others. In Jesus's name, amen.

Prayer for Ethical Dilemmas

Father, we are facing situations that challenge our values and convictions. Give us the courage to do what is right even when it is difficult or costly. Help us be people of integrity who honor You in all our decisions. Show us how to navigate these challenges in ways that reflect Your character and serve Your purposes. In Jesus's name, amen.

Prayer for Leadership Transitions

Lord, as leadership changes on this project, we pray for continuity and stability during the transition. Help new leaders understand the vision and build on the foundation that has been laid. Give wisdom to outgoing leaders as they transfer knowledge and relationships. May this change ultimately serve the project and all stakeholders well. In Jesus's name, amen.

Prayer for Remote Teams

Heavenly Father, our team is distributed across different locations, making communication and collaboration more challenging. Help us build strong relationships despite the physical distance. Give us patience with technology limitations and wisdom in how we communicate. Create unity of purpose and spirit among all team members. In Jesus's name, amen.

Legacy and Mentoring Prayers

Prayer for Legacy

Father, help me build a legacy that honors You and serves others. May the people I lead be better because of our time together. May the organizations I serve be strengthened through my contributions. May the Kingdom work be advanced through my faithful stewardship. Use my life and work for Your glory and purposes. In Jesus's name, amen.

Prayer for Mentoring

Lord, You have placed people in my path who need guidance and encouragement in their leadership development. Help me be a faithful mentor who invests in their growth and success. Give me wisdom to know what they need and patience to support them through challenges. Use our relationship to prepare them for greater service to You. In Jesus's name, amen.

Prayer for Mentors

Heavenly Father, thank You for the mentors You have provided in my life and career. Bless those who have invested in my development and continue to guide my growth. Help me honor their investment by serving others well and mentoring the next generation as they have mentored me. In Jesus's name, amen.

Prayer for the Next Generation

Lord, I pray for the emerging leaders who will take over project management responsibilities in the future. Prepare them for the challenges they will face and the opportunities they will have to serve. Help us create environments where they can learn and grow. Use each of us to prepare the way for more effective Kingdom service. In Jesus's name, amen.

How to Use These Prayers (Where Appropriate, in Holy Spirit Discernment)

Personal Devotion

- Begin each day with appropriate morning prayers.
- Use midday prayers to refocus during busy periods.
- End workdays with evening prayers of gratitude and reflection.

Team Integration

- Open team meetings with brief, inclusive prayers when appropriate.
- Use project phase prayers at major milestones.
- Encourage team members to share prayer requests related to work challenges.

Crisis Response

- Turn immediately to challenge prayers when difficulties arise.
- Involve your personal prayer network in significant project challenges.
- Use prayer as a tool for maintaining perspective during high-stress periods.

Celebration and Learning

- Include prayers of thanksgiving in project closure activities.
- Use success prayers to maintain humility during achievements.
- Incorporate prayer into lessons learned and reflection processes.

Leadership Development

- Pray regularly for people you are mentoring or developing.
- Use prayer as a tool for seeking wisdom in leadership decisions.
- Model dependence on God through visible prayer practices.

Remember, prayer is not a substitute for competent project management. It's the foundation that makes competent project management a form of worship and service to God.

About the Author

Shawna Calhoun is a seasoned project management professional with over 20 years of experience across healthcare, biotech, education, and a brief venture into oil and gas. Currently serving in a remote leadership role for a major healthcare organization, she blends technical expertise with spiritual insight to lead with clarity and purpose. Holding a bachelor's in IT, an MBA in Project Management, PMP certification, and multiple Agile credentials, Shawna is also a respected instructor, consultant, speaker, and mentor. She volunteers with PMI, contributes to university advisory boards, and is pursuing her DBA in Project Management. Born again in 2019, Shawna's testimony is one of perseverance—overcoming personal trials including trauma, divorce, job loss, and profound betrayal. She's gifted in "connecting the dots," often drawing connections between Scripture and professional principles, such as those found in The 7 Habits of Highly Effective People. Her leadership encourages others to live a fruitful faith-forward life with wisdom and grace in Christ.

www.ingramcontent.com/pod-product-compliance
Lightning Source LLC
Chambersburg PA
CBHW070605170426
43200CB00012B/2592